D0455094

The
FUTURE
of
STRATEGY

A Transformative Approach to Strategy for a World That Won't Stand Still

Johan Aurik • Martin Fabel • Gillis Jonk

NEW YORK   CHICAGO   SAN FRANCISCO
ATHENS   LONDON   MADRID
MEXICO CITY   MILAN   NEW DELHI
SINGAPORE   SYDNEY   TORONTO

1 2 3 4 5 6 7 8 9 0   DOC/DOC   1 2 0 9 8 7 6 5 4

ISBN   978-0-07-184874-9
MHID   0-07-184874-6

e-ISBN   978-0-07-184875-6
e-MHID   0-07-184875-4

McGraw-Hill Education books are available at special quantity discounts to use as premiums and sales promotions or for use in corporate training programs. To contact a representative, please visit the Contact Us pages at www.mhprofessional.com.

Throughout our careers we have been extraordinarily fortunate to learn from, work beside, and partner with the best. We gratefully dedicate this book to our mentors, colleagues, and clients who have inspired us to dig deeper and reach higher—challenging the status quo, always with the goal of making things better.

Contents

Acknowledgments

W E BEGAN THINKING ABOUT WRITING a strategy book in 2012, inspired by the many challenges that our clients were facing. Just like today, companies were struggling with more competitive markets and trends that were forcing smaller players out of business and leading bigger players to alter, and even shorten, their strategies. How do you deliberate over five- or ten-year strategies when your markets are being shaken by a bright new technology every six months? How do you stick to a long-term plan when an upstart challenger is doing everything faster, better, and cheaper than you are?

We had answers for these challenges, thanks to decades of research and experience working with organizations in most industries. But writing a book is never the work of just one, two, or three people. Our colleagues helped us by sharing their own expertise from their work with clients. This book incorporates our insights, learnings, and hands-on experience as well as those of our colleagues: Carol Cruickshank, Adam Dixon, Saurine Doshi, Richard Forrest, Laurent Guerard, Martin Handschuh, Angus Hodgson, Andres Mendoza Pena, Naveen Menon, Isabel Neiva, Joe Reifel, Sean Ryan, Priscilla Seki, Tak Umezawa, and Zuwairi Zakaria.

Steve Denning provided valuable support and expertise, becoming a sounding board for new perspectives and concepts. Patricia Sibo and Sharon Putman handled the overall revisions with great patience and professionalism, and, of course, we are grateful to Knox Huston at McGraw-Hill for his enthusiastic support and close cooperation.

Introduction

ONE OF US WAS HAVING DINNER some time ago when a colleague asked him why he didn't play chess. "All strategists play chess," his colleague said, "so why don't you?" Everyone at the table was silent, waiting for an answer.

Years ago, our colleague would have had a point. In the 1980s, strategy was indeed like playing chess, which is done on a board with 64 squares and 6 unique pieces, or chessmen, that are allowed specific moves. Chess and strategy were about thinking ahead and anticipating competitors' moves. Each could be done in a fairly analytical way, drawing on what had happened in the past. That IBM's supercomputer Watson was able to beat Gary Kasparov, the world's best chess player in the 1990s, is evidence of this.

Today, strategy is very different. Imagine playing chess on a board that gets bigger in some areas, but smaller in others. You don't know where it will grow or shrink, or whether growth will occur in squares, circles, or triangles. Imagine that the number of pieces also changes. You can split pieces in two or merge them, and some pieces can become obsolete. On top of that, new moves are allowed—rooks start jumping, and knights can run across the board. Some parts of the board vanish and new opportunities pop up, allowing your mutating stable of pieces to move in new and attractive ways, and, to top it off, more players start playing on your board.

Strategy today is about more than analyzing and anticipating predefined moves and thinking several moves ahead. It is also about determining where interesting opportunities for creating strategic advantage will arise, where new rules can work to your advantage, where the playing field might expand or contract, and where new threats might appear. It is also about how—how new pieces can help create or defend strategic advantage, and how to determine it is time to abandon once-promising game plans. Analytics won't solve today's problems, which is one reason why twenty-first-century strategy isn't like playing chess.

The Trouble with Strategy

In the past, business leaders turned to strategy to set the direction of the business and help them make choices amid the chaos. After all, for thousands of years, ever since Sun Tzu wrote *The Art of War*, strategy has been about finding a path to success amid uncertainty and complexity.

But today, strategy in business has fallen into disrepute. The expensive large-scale strategic planning exercises that were common in the late twentieth century are no longer perceived as providing commensurate returns in terms of contributing to the firm's success. They were more useful in evaluating strategies in the rearview mirror than in generating value going forward. What really sealed the fate of these exercises was the fast-changing, increasingly dynamic and complex business environment.

Everywhere executives look there are vast possibilities for doing things faster, cheaper, and better. However, they find it increasingly difficult to predict where their business or industry is heading and which companies will succeed. Organizations are chasing competitive advantage from multiple sources indiscriminately, with initiatives sometimes operating at cross-purposes. Not surprisingly, the returns on these initiatives, even if they could be implemented, are increasingly meager. One CEO told us, "Everybody is working extremely hard, and we believe that we are doing the right things—but so are all of our competitors. The situation has become impossible."

During all of this, strategy has taken a backseat. In our latest strategy survey, almost half of the respondents considered organizational *agility* to be at least as important as strategy, and a third believed that agility *is* what strategy is about.

Those Big Strategic Planning Exercises

With companies facing growing competition, an abundance of opportunities, and an unpredictable future, strategic planning exercises proved to be ill equipped to keep up. For example, it was fine to talk in strategy sessions about moving to "blue oceans," but in the real world, managers could see only shark-infested "red oceans." It was no longer enough to offer products that were either better or cheaper than competitors' or more customized to a narrow market segment. Suddenly, success depended on delivering products that were better *and* cheaper *and* more tailored.

Strategic planning exercises also had trouble predicting or defending against disruption of the kind described in Clayton Christensen's *The Innovator's Dilemma* as "initially-inferior cheaper products that eventually improved and took over your high-value customers." These exercises were even less able to cope with more profound disruptions, where entire product lines or markets were obliterated as customers defected en masse and flocked to a product or service that was at once better, cheaper, quicker, smaller, more personalized, *and* more convenient.

And the typical setup for strategy did not help. Strategy was conceived of as an esoteric high-altitude activity, moving from the ivory tower down to the workers below, and as a result, it failed to take advantage of the valuable firsthand knowledge that workers have of customers, competitors, processes, and suppliers. The handover from the group that developed the strategy to the people who were expected to execute it led to a disconnect in implementation. Research by John P. Kotter puts the failure rate of top-driven change management initiatives at 70 percent[1]—a steep discount on a company's brightest ideas.

Then there is the innate bias toward inaction. The massive strategic planning exercises tended to alarm decision makers as they contemplated the risks, difficulties, and dislocations of undertaking major change. All too often, the outcome was to conclude that change was too risky. Even firms like Nokia, Xerox, and Kodak, which had accurately predicted what was to come, "fumbled the future" and let competitors steal the advantage.

Strategy's failure at coping with a different and uncertain future kept companies locked up in the here and now and dealing with everything that was thrown at them. There was a price to pay for this. As organizations lost sight of their objectives, their common sense of purpose slowly eroded until financial performance became the overriding goal.

Back to Basics: What Is Strategy?

At A.T. Kearney, we believe that a game change is required to get companies out of the vicious cycle of busy thinking, frenetic activity, and bureaucratic planning and enable them to deal with their strategic challenges effectively. Strategy, when properly understood and executed, has never been more important. Strategy is the art and science by which managers use their authority to accomplish the organization's mission—to assess the current situation, anticipate the future, direct the actions of employees, seize opportunities, and cope with competitors. It is through strategy that managers initiate, influence, and synchronize the activities of the organization.

Lessons from the Military

Most books on business strategy acknowledge the military origins of strategy. Yet by the nineteenth century, military thinkers had realized that big strategic plans developed at the top didn't work on a complex, fast-moving battlefield where the enemy kept doing unexpected things. So military strategy evolved to encompass more dynamic approaches, focused on strategic thinking, action, and involvement.

Business strategy, meanwhile, went off on a tangent toward the big top-down plans. By the end of the 1960s, when business strategy had become a proper discipline with its own practitioners, tools, and methodologies, the approach to strategy was modeled on its direct precursor, scientific management, instead of taking inspiration from its conceptual military parent.

This book is about pulling back from that misguided tangent and returning strategy to its rightful place as the overarching management system. We take the lessons from the military and build on them, applying them not only to strategy deployment but also to strategy formulation (see the sidebar "Detailed Command Versus Mission Command").

Our inspiration for doing so is derived from what A.T. Kearney has accomplished. Strategy, when rightly conceived and executed, integrates the activities of the other management systems. It is a resource multiplier. By eliminating initiatives that don't fit the future game plan, strategy frees up resources that can be refocused on initiatives that support the strategic vision.

DETAILED COMMAND VERSUS MISSION COMMAND

The U.S. Army, in its formal theory of warfare, contrasts "detailed command" with "mission command." Conceptually, these reflect two different approaches to dealing with uncertainty.

Detailed command is focused on information and data. It aims to reduce uncertainty within the ranks of the upper echelon by collecting more and better data and by increasing the information processing capability. It trades speed for completeness of information. It often results in greater uncertainty at the lower levels because people at these levels do not have the information on which decisions are based and therefore are not committed to those decisions. As a result, implementation requires greater control of lower-level managers and more detailed orders, which in turn limit the creativity that staff members can contribute.

Because of the difficulty of getting accurate, up-to-date information about the situation on the ground, and because of the gap between conception and execution, the appearance of more certainty at the top is often an illusion.

Mission command is action-oriented. It aims at reducing uncertainty evenly throughout the organization. Leaders educate their organizations to codevelop a widely understood strategic vision and manage a set of strategic missions as part of normal operations. They delegate authority for decision making to those levels that can acquire and process information and move into action quickly without waiting for detailed orders. The process makes full use of the organization's talent.

The mission command approach to strategy leads to a more flexible approach to management, leading to a greater understanding throughout the organization and, overall, a more agile and effective organization.

While the two approaches are a continuum, not a dichotomy, it is important to recognize that in the twentieth-century military, the conduct of operations steadily shifted from information-based strategy to mission command strategy. In the military, detailed command is increasingly being seen as appropriate for technical and procedural tasks, while mission command is viewed as the more appropriate approach to the actual conduct of military operations.

FutureProof Strategy:
A New Way of Conducting Strategy

FutureProof strategy is our core approach to carrying out strategic management at all levels of the organization. We synthesize three powerful principles that, *in combination*, set ours apart from all other approaches to strategy:

- *Draw inspiration from the future.* The emphasis shifts from focusing on research, analyses, and extrapolations of current issues to looking to the future for strategic inspiration and purpose. Instead of piling on ever more complicated analyses to understand what's happening now, strategic thinking takes direct cues from fundamental trends that are affecting the company now or could affect the company in the future. Doing this helps protect the firm from unexpected developments. There is another advantage: megabytes of analyses do not necessarily lead to inspiration, whereas fundamental trends supported by examples, facts, figures, and stories do.

- *Be organizationally inclusive.* A good strategy is not created in isolation at the top and cascaded down through the organization. Instead, an effective strategy is one that is organizationally comprehensive, engaging people across and up and down the company in formulating it. It provides the multidisciplinary capacity to translate fundamental trends into relevant opportunities for creating competitive advantage and then deploys the appropriate initiatives. And our FutureProof approach effectively eliminates the handover hurdle between formulation and execution, one of the major reasons for strategy failure.

- *Take a portfolio approach.* Competitive advantage has an increasingly brief lifespan, which means that companies need to not only devise more competitive opportunities, but also manage them on an ongoing life-cycle basis. When some of these opportunities have run their course, others must be ready to take over to keep the organization at the competitive edge of the market. Rather than thinking of strategy as a single perfect plan with a multiyear deployment cycle, we think in terms of a portfolio of competitive opportunities. The opportunities are connected by an overall strategic game plan and are continually grown and culled by people within the organization. In this way, the firm's activities stay aligned with its competitive goals and in sync with fast-changing business environments.

Enacting these three principles requires a certain leap of faith. It requires courage to look to the future rather than the present, to include many people across the company in the strategy development process, and to turn logic and a portfolio of competitive goals into a living, guiding strategic framework for the organization.

FutureProof strategy has a number of advantages over more traditional strategy approaches, allowing an organization to:

- Formulate strategies for creating and capturing value.

- Extend strategic control by turning strategy from a single solution into a guiding strategic framework.

- Make the strategy process truly transformational.

- Overcome a bias toward inaction.

And, above all:

- Provide a framework for dealing with uncertainty—balancing strategic direction and guidance with organizational agility.

Yet, while all three principles have clear benefits, each one by itself has significant drawbacks. For example, a *focus on the future* may inspire an organization, but unless many knowledgeable people are included, it won't catch fire. And if the focus is not grounded in solid analyses, it may very well lead to misguided decisions. An *organizationally inclusive* approach to strategy formulation can eradicate the massive change management hurdle between corner-office conception and rank-and-file execution, but such engagement can become a glorified corporate suggestion box if it is not carefully guided and inspired. Finally, while a *portfolio approach* to competitive advantage can provide ongoing flexibility, unless the portfolio is filled with distinct, deeply analyzed, and mutually reinforcing opportunities, it is just an empty tool.

With this in mind, we believe not only that it is *possible* to combine these principles, but that it is *necessary* to do so to mitigate their individual drawbacks. Indeed, in combination, the sum is greater than the parts.

- *Inspiration*, when carefully selected, provides *inclusiveness* with the necessary guidance and focus to ensure a relevant outcome.

- *Inclusion* provides *inspiration* with the necessary capacity to tackle the most challenging issues and opportunities holistically. It also paves the way for implementation.

- A *portfolio* allows the output of *inspiration* and *inclusiveness* to be turned into a guiding strategic framework for the entire organization—one that can be grown and maintained on an ongoing basis.

The Challenge: Creating and Capturing Value

A successful strategy provides a company with more opportunities to be innovative and more ways to delight customers. The challenge is how to extract value from these opportunities. Organizations that focus only on delighting customers often end up in a death spiral. They may temporarily please customers with a new and innovative product, but they then fail to extract value from the innovations because they lack the means to do so. Having more opportunities to innovate also creates more ways to capture value. Many things have to fall into place for the value of the whole to become truly "advantaged"—in other words, for the whole to be greater than the sum of its parts.

The pharmaceutical industry has long been a model of extreme value creation and capture. Using R&D to find new ways to lessen human suffering creates value at a societal level; patent-protected delivery of this value ensures commensurate returns.

Apple is another value leader. The company provides value holistically: through iTunes, its App Store, the design of its hardware, its operating and functional software, and its brand identity. Apple turns this into a hardware life cycle measured in years with an absolute minimum number of product variants—something that was previously unheard of in the high-tech industry. This allows Apple to benefit from exceptional economies of scale and deliver products that provide extraordinary margins.

Volkswagen also captures value through economies of scale, but in a different way. The automaker offers a wide range of vehicles under multiple brands to meet the tastes and spending power of different customers. At the back end, Volkswagen has one of the most effective platforms for designing and manufacturing cars through the reuse of components, subassemblies, and platforms.

Walmart is another example. The world's largest retailer, employing more than a million people in North America alone, uses its size advantage to help its customers "save money, live better." Walmart can price products so attractively that it can draw in the numbers of consumers needed to give it revenues of $475 billion and still make a very respectable return on sales. What's more, over the past few years, the company has put its pure size and scale to work to push the envelope on sustainable business practices.

Brands provide another way to capture value. Coca-Cola, one of the most valuable brands in the world, is extremely effective at maintaining its brand as a continued source of competitive advantage.

Even within a single industry, there can be different approaches to capturing value. Microsoft used to sell software—both operating software and functional software. Gradually it is shifting part of its offering to a subscription model similar to that of Salesforce.com. Apple, on the other hand, provides a lot of software either for free or for a very modest price, knowing that it will make up the difference through hardware sales. And Amazon makes most of its revenue from media content (books, videos, and music), with hardware (such as the Kindle) being sold at cost or for a loss as a way to promote the sale of content.

These examples illustrate that there is no one-size-fits-all approach to extracting value. What's important is that the approach has merit, and that all parts of the company are involved. This is why strategy must be released from its C-suite confines and made truly *inclusive*. Knowledge and expertise from different parts of the organization help determine the recipes for capturing value and shape an understanding of what the different parts are capable of contributing. As individual products or services are managed within the firm's overall strategic logic, value must be captured across the entire offering. At the same time, a *portfolio approach* to managing multiple competitive opportunities ensures organizational alignment and reinforces efforts to bring the chosen strategy to life.

Expanding Strategic Control

Traditional top-down strategy gives the impression of control. It allows the leaders to make all the necessary high-level trade-offs for the organization and consider a variety of boundary conditions. The leaders also work on formulating a strategy (a strategy, by the way, that is often formulated without firsthand information regarding markets, customers, processes, or capabilities) until it is ready to be passed on to the organization for execution.

However, control where it really matters—in execution—is often lacking. What good is 100 percent control over strategic instructions that are increasingly flawed or irrelevant and will at best be only partially executed? In a 2013 A.T. Kearney study, we asked some 2,000 executives and senior managers about their companies' strategies and their ability to deliver results. More than 80 percent of C-suite executives said that their strategies at least met all expectations and surpassed some or all of them, while close to 50 percent of senior managers said that the same strategies had failed to deliver on at least some of their expectations (see Figure I.1).

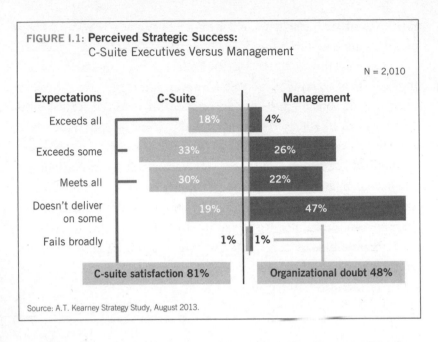

FIGURE I.1: **Perceived Strategic Success:**
C-Suite Executives Versus Management

N = 2,010

Source: A.T. Kearney Strategy Study, August 2013.

The whole notion of control deserves rethinking. Rather than being created by issuing detailed instructions, control works best when it encapsulates the sharing of information to influence the conception and execution of strategy. Strategy then is multidirectional, with feedback influencing managers from below, from above, and laterally. Strategy directs the practice and organization of control, while control informs the exercise of strategy and regulates the functions of the organization.

True Change Requires Transformation

A proper strategy implies at least some change for the organization. This means that strategy itself has to be transformational, working from different assumptions about what constitutes competitive advantage to bring about true change.

This is where FutureProof strategy comes into play. The organization has to change its perception of reality, discarding or adapting at least some of its ingrained and often subconscious assumptions about how its business, customers, markets, and processes work. It starts with *inspiration* in the form of identifying fundamental trends that will be decisive for the company's future competitiveness. Assessing the implications of such trends helps the company's leaders rethink at least some of their core assumptions and set the strategic direction. With *inclusiveness*, the wider organization is able to reconsider these core assumptions, educate itself, and become better at anticipating change.

Take Nintendo, the maker of handheld computer games and consoles. For a long time, the core assumption in the gaming industry was that the graphical quality of a game was crucial for its success. This drove an arms race for better and more expensive graphical processes and more graphically detailed games. Nintendo challenged this core assumption, figuring out that for a large number of potential consumers, the physical game interface was a more exciting feature than the graphical interface. The result was the Nintendo Wii—a game console that had very basic graphics (and thus was cost-effective to produce, even in-house), but also had controllers and motion sensors that allowed gamers to stand in front of televisions to golf, ski, and play tennis. The Wii console was sold out for years after its introduction.

Nintendo is unusual. Most firms still operate within the existing rules and assumptions of their sectors. FutureProof strategy rises above the constraints of the existing situation, creating a new situation with new rules and dramatically improved outcomes. Sectors that appeared to be mature or moribund suddenly become growth sectors that are full of promise. Given today's fast-changing and dynamic business environment, it is clear that more future-focused, inclusive strategies are required.

FutureProof Strategy

A successful strategy rests on the following:

- A powerful guiding portfolio of competitive opportunities developed in an organizationally inclusive manner.

- Organizational ownership and the ability to be creative within the framework of strategic guidance.

- A "fit" established between (1) strategic guidance and the current situation, (2) the constraints facing the organization, and (3) evolving future events; resources are then allocated in accordance with the strategic guidance.

- A culture of trust and mutual respect.

The conceptually distinct approaches of analysis- and research-based strategic planning on the one hand and FutureProof strategy on the other represent the theoretical extremes of strategy (see Figure I.2). In practice, no manager relies purely on detailed strategic plans or purely on inclusiveness. While the demands of today's marketplace usually require inclusive strategy, the degree to which managers incorporate analysis-centric techniques into their strategic management practices depends on various factors—the nature of the envi-

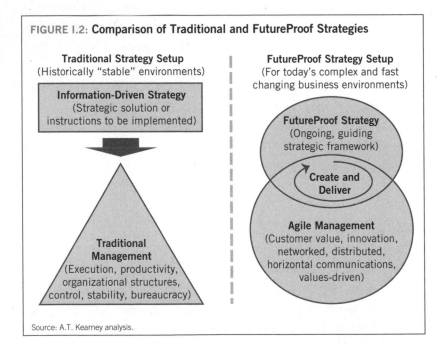

FIGURE I.2: **Comparison of Traditional and FutureProof Strategies**

Traditional Strategy Setup
(Historically "stable" environments)

Information-Driven Strategy
(Strategic solution or instructions to be implemented)

Traditional Management
(Execution, productivity, organizational structures, control, stability, bureaucracy)

FutureProof Strategy Setup
(For today's complex and fast changing business environments)

FutureProof Strategy
(Ongoing, guiding strategic framework)

Create and Deliver

Agile Management
(Customer value, innovation, networked, distributed, horizontal communications, values-driven)

Source: A.T. Kearney analysis.

ronment, the task at hand, the qualities of the staff and managers, the capabilities of competitors, and governance imposed by the leaders or the regulatory environment.

Looking Ahead

In Chapter 1, we describe the principle of *drawing inspiration from the future*. We show how strategic thinking takes direct cues from fundamental trends that are on the horizon and creates a strategic game plan that can inspire the entire organization.

Chapter 2 explains the principle of *organizational inclusiveness*, with strategic cocreation that engages many people from across the company—sometimes everyone—in formulating it. This approach generates the capacity to take on the competitive opportunities and eliminates one of the major reasons for strategy failure: the handover hurdle between formulation and execution.

In Chapter 3, we cover the *portfolio approach*. With competitive advantages having an increasingly brief life cycle, firms must learn how to manage a portfolio of competitive opportunities within a relatively stable strategic game plan. We explain how to manage these opportunities on an ongoing, life-cycle basis. When some of them have run their course, new ones are ready to take over. The portfolio must be grown and culled continually by people within the organization.

Chapter 4 looks at how these *three principles come together* in a single approach. We look in more detail at how one financial services firm put the three principles together so that in combination, the result of the principles was greater than the sum of its parts. By so doing, the firm injects inspiration, opportunity, and energy into the organization.

In Chapter 5, we explore the issues involved in FutureProof strategy, and how any organization can use this approach to overcome seemingly overwhelming constraints and *transform its future*.

In Chapter 6, we outline ways in which strategy can help a company deal with *competitive threats and the various forms of disruption*.

Finally, Chapter 7 discusses how to *get started* in reclaiming strategy, doing so while overcoming the bias toward inaction and maintaining the status quo.

Clients tell us that, with our approach to strategy, their employees are better able to identify competitive advantages that can be tapped quickly and threats that need to be avoided or blocked. These organizations have started to regain the flexibility necessary to make ongoing adjustments in the face of changing circumstances—something that is accomplished when the entire organization is thinking and acting strategically.

Strategy is no longer a periodically run, burdensome direction-setting exercise, but rather an ongoing source of organizational inspiration and energy. Rather than being whipsawed by constant change, managers are better able to foresee and take advantage of what's coming, and to align the organization accordingly. For leaders of companies who've felt as if they're barely keeping up, this is the best news of all.

CHAPTER 1

Drawing Inspiration from the Future

In 2004, when I was writing my book The Earth Is Flat, *Facebook didn't make the index. Twitter was a sound. The cloud was something in the sky. 4G was a parking place. LinkedIn was a prison. For most people, applications were what you sent to college, and Skype was a typo.*

—THOMAS FRIEDMAN[1]

To BELIEVE THAT YOU HAVE the perfect strategy and that you are secure no matter what may happen in the future is to adopt a rigid, static position that will be your undoing. The illusion that it is possible to use strategy to insulate an organization from the future has regularly been seen in military history. Bows and arrows defeat swords. Cavalry defeats infantry. Rifles defeat bows and arrows. Machine guns defeat rifles. Tanks defeat machine guns. And so on.

When a superior military technology comes along, resisting it is futile. People often cling to the familiar, thinking that if they put in a little more effort, they can preserve the old way of doing things. They stick to the past until their losses are so great that they must either admit defeat and move into the future or be annihilated.

Similar phenomena occur in free enterprise economies. Except where government regulation or private monopolies preserve the status quo, the emergence of a new technology or methodology sparks a process of creative destruction: more progressive firms adopt the new ways and push those that hang on to the status quo out of business. As in military affairs, resisting this process is futile.[2]

Forward-thinking players avoid taking the view that the overall goal of strategy is to *protect* the organization *against* the future. This is the wrong mindset for strategy. Instead, the goal of strategy is to *align* the organization *with* the future and *take advantage* of it. Strategic gains come from collaborating with and profiting from the future, not from fighting it or resisting it. In strategy, the future is a friend, not an enemy.

The Impact of Fundamental Trends

For many managers, there's never been a more frightening time to be in business. With so many initiatives and opportunities being pursued in so many different directions, executives are finding it increasingly difficult to predict where things are heading and who will be successful with what and when.

The trigger for this is easy to see. Over the past two decades, the number of fundamental trends has multiplied, creating a wealth of opportunities to do things differently. Technological advancement—and the almost unlimited possibilities that it brings—is well documented. Businesses and value chains can be configured in new ways as we outsource, insource, partner, acquire, merge, divest, cobrand, codevelop, and cocreate. Talent is on the move, as people are no longer convinced that lifelong careers can provide the most relevant professional challenges. And then, of course, there are the usual suspects of globalization, deregulation, and economic uncertainty.

The profound impact of these and other fundamental trends on business is evident in three kinds of strategic challenges:

1. Doing more of the same, but with a lot more urgency.   The first challenge is a sharp acceleration in the process of improving products and services. Customers expect to have everything they want whenever they want it and wherever they are. They want to be in control and to have support that is always available but never intrusive. They expect transparency and convenience, and they want it all for the lowest possible price—preferably free. Power in the marketplace has made an unprecedented shift to consumers, who are not shy about making demands.

For the most part, companies have tried to deliver on customers' expectations by doing more of the same, but with a lot more urgency. Technology was there to help speed things up, an acceleration that is most striking in software development. Microsoft used to upgrade its Office program every couple of years, and Salesforce.com issues upgrades several times a year. But newer businesses such as Etsy issue smaller upgrades *every day*. A free enterprise system's tilt toward creative destruction then takes over: Knowledge can't be put back in the bottle. Once customers know that it is possible for companies to operate better and faster, they expect nothing less, and it becomes the new normal. Except where government regulation or private monopolies preserve the status quo, firms that don't adjust don't survive.

An insurance firm might reply: "None of this applies to us. You are talking about software. Insurance is different." This response ignores the fact that most firms' core systems and processes already depend on software. It also overlooks the likelihood that within a few years, the insurance industry will be much more digitized, virtualized, and hands-on (in real time), and will entirely run on software.

The hospitality industry is in the same boat. A few years ago, hospitality was mostly about prime real estate, efficient housekeeping, good food, friendly front desk personnel, and providing an exceptional guest experience. Then the online upstarts got into the game. Booking.com, Expedia, and TripAdvisor.com (to name just three) took a material share of profits, while peer-to-peer rental platforms such as Airbnb and HomeAway created an altogether new class of competitors.

This challenge comes with a risk. For most companies, the additional workload created by the accelerated process for improving products and services is already substantial, often bordering on over-burdening.

"Let's admit it," management expert Gary Hamel wrote almost two decades ago. "Corporations around the world are reaching the limits of incrementalism. Squeezing another penny out of costs, getting a product to market a few weeks earlier, responding to customers' inquiries a little bit faster, ratcheting quality up one more notch, capturing another point of market share—these are the obsessions of managers today. But pursuing incremental improvements while rivals reinvent the industry is like fiddling while Rome burns."[3]

2. Not only with more urgency, but differently.   Whole business sectors are not just becoming faster, cheaper, or simply better with more urgency. They are becoming *different* as the vast possibilities for finding new ways of doing things are required by customers and exploited by alert producers.

Our earlier examples of Booking.com and Expedia illustrate how the process of dis- and re-intermediation continues with comparison websites, online auctions, and secondhand-goods sites. Classified advertising sections in newspapers have been annihilated. The music industry is just now seeing modest growth after two decades of decline. Yet it is still not even half of what it was at its peak in 1999.

Online sales channels are also affected. Amazon increased the assortment available at a bookstore from a healthy 70,000 titles to several million, along with all sorts of subscriptions and streamed music. Configurability of products is similarly pervasive: we now configure our own personal computers, kitchens, and even clothing without giving it much thought.

Customer service has gone through a major transformation. People no longer turn to manufacturers when they run into problems; they turn to consumer groups such as the Apple user community or the digital photography forums on dpreview.com that provide information and troubleshooting advice much faster. Indeed, entire processes have been handed over to consumers. Look at air travel. The only encounters with real people are likely to be those with the security guards and the flight crew handing out drinks and snacks. Travelers do the rest, from booking the flight and choosing seats to getting boarding passes and checking luggage.

As a result, business models have changed. Amazon still sells books and music, but it also makes good money as a virtual shopping mall and an e-commerce "shared service and logistics center" that rents out virtual shops and handles third-party orders and all sorts of web services.

The challenge with doing things differently is that there is no limit to the number of opportunities, and this comes on top of the need to deal with the faster process for improving products and services.

The risk here is that the "incumbent" parts of the business are so overwhelmed by the urgency of doing things differently that they have no capacity to keep an eye out for the third type of challenge: doing things disruptively differently.

3. Doing things disruptively differently.   The third category of strategic challenge goes beyond both being more urgent and being different; it *disrupts* even seemingly robust businesses. This disruption can come in the form of a new product or service that makes an incumbent abruptly less relevant. For example, physical navigation devices lost all their momentum within a year or two. When Google Maps appeared, as Larry Downes and Paul Nunes explain in *Big Bang Disruption*, it was free, more accurate, and more convenient. The result? It put the global market for stand-alone navigation devices in reverse, shrinking it from its peak of 33 million units in 2011 to 28 million in 2012.[4,5]

In fact, Downes and Nunes offer a long list of products that have become, or are rapidly becoming, less relevant:

Address books, video cameras, pagers, wristwatches, maps, books, travel games, flashlights, home telephones, dictation machines, cash registers, Walkmans, Day-Timers, alarm clocks, answering machines, yellow pages, wallets, keys, phrase books, transistor radios, personal digital assistants, dashboard navigation systems, remote controls, airline ticket counters, newspapers and magazines, directory assistance, travel and insurance agents, restaurant guides, and pocket calculators.[6]

One of the most famous disruptors is Moore's law. Named after a former Intel CEO, Moore's law says that the number of transistors on a microprocessor doubles every 18 to 24 months. And since the growth is exponential, we have to imagine what electronics will be able to do for us when these devices are 20 times more useful (which will happen in less than a decade)—something that we are not very good at.

Then there is the network effect. If Facebook is a proxy for a network of 1.1 billion people created in less than a decade, how will this fast-growing network capitalize on 20 times more useful electronics? Cell phones and smartphones have seen an equally impressive trajectory. From Autotel to GSM, GPRS, EDGE, UMTS, 3G, and now 4G, things have become not just better, but drastically better. Many of these exponential trends reinforce each other. So as connectivity allows us to make greater use of our smartphones, we are better able to exploit the networks that we create.

Clearly, the speed with which these fundamental trends change makes it more difficult to assess their impact, especially when they interact. So any measure of control or ability to positively influence disruption should be pursued.

Fundamental Trends as Solutions

We have to be smarter about the trends that bring about such disruption. We know, for example, that not all trends are linear and independent. Fundamental trends also interact. And as more trends—especially the exponential ones—interact, they drive unprecedented change. If fundamental trends are making our business lives more dynamic and complex, it is only logical that we turn to them for a solution. Fortunately, they have a characteristic that makes them manageable: *individual trends are mostly relatively stable and can be understood and harnessed.* That's because they are often long-lasting and directionally consistent over time. For many of them, the implications and impact have already become apparent in other sectors or countries.

Social media? Using online networks to connect seamlessly started in earnest less than a decade ago and will not be phased out anytime soon. The Internet? It has been a major force in reducing interaction costs between people and businesses and will continue to be such a force for decades to come. Networked business models? We have decades' worth of experience and a lot of untapped potential. Demographic change and aging populations have been coming slowly and predictably, but the transformational implications are just beginning.

Many of the business dynamics and urgencies we are experiencing today are not the result of unpredictable, sudden, or fast-moving individual trends. Rather, they come from the *simultaneous effect* of these trends on our businesses, markets, and operations. Their combination creates more opportunities than we can capitalize on. And because we all pursue different opportunities, one company's successful pursuit is another company's sudden and urgent need to catch up—thus fueling even more complexity and urgency.

This insight offers an important clue for designing a practical, prospective approach to reclaiming strategy: *we can get a better grip on our future by understanding the long-lasting, directionally stable individual trends, especially the most disruptive ones.*

Future-Focused Versus Traditional Business Strategy

An understanding of what will drive change in the future cannot be arrived at through traditional approaches to strategy development. Consider our insurance company again. With traditional strategic planning, an insurance firm that sells much of its product through brokers might analyze the broker market, determine its market share in various segments, figure out what other insurance companies are doing in each segment, evaluate significant trends, and then formulate a strategy based on the results.

A future-focused strategy switches the order around. It evaluates the most significant trends, asking the relevant "what-if" questions and drawing on the experience of, for example, other countries and sectors. Based on this, it's not difficult to figure out that insurance will soon be fully digitized. Customers will get the bulk of their advice from virtual knowledge and smart applications, rendering perhaps 80 percent of brokers' traditional activities and services superfluous.

Recognizing this, the firm can begin to understand its business situation from a "future-in" perspective and evaluate which brokers are likely to come out on top. And it might find that today's most demanding, difficult-to-serve brokers are the ones who are making the most progress in providing their customers with the most convenient digital experiences.

Thinking in terms of individual trends facilitates the process of formulating and implementing strategy. For insurance, the competitive bar is being raised because of major opportunities to shift costs out of the insurance value chain while also increasing value to customers. This is compounded by a growing transparency. Fortunately, the same trends that create this situation also provide the opportunity to take the value proposition for customers to the next level.

Abductive Logic and FutureProof Strategy

Inherent in this process is assessing the implications of the most relevant trends for customers, the company, the competition, and operations. This assessment is not based on traditional inductive or deductive logic: "Is it true?" or "Can I prove that?" Rather, it is based on abductive reasoning, a kind of logic pioneered by American philosopher Charles Sanders Peirce and discussed in Roger Martin's book *The Design of Business: Why Design Thinking Is the Next Competitive Advantage.*[7]

The questions for strategists are:

- Might this become true?

- How likely is it to become true?

- What will follow if it becomes true?

- What things would have to happen for this to become true?

- How feasible are those things?

Does this abductive logic mean the end of analysis as it was practiced in traditional strategy exercises? Not at all. We still need competitive analyses to substantiate the trends and make them as convincing, irrefutable, and inspirational as possible—to create a sort of competitive baseline. But we need to change the order in which this is done. Now, strategic insights are derived from the trends and competitive analysis is used to validate them.

Doing so helps to overcome the inherent bias that is present in data analyses. Data are biased toward the present over the future, and toward the known over the unknown. In a faster-changing and more dynamic environment, this bias impedes the effectiveness of data analysis as a source of strategic insight.

Overcoming this bias requires first overcoming major obstacles, which Roger Martin describes as essential to getting a productive balance between analytical and abductive thinking. The following obstacles are described in Martin's book *The Design of Business: Why Design Thinking Is the Next Competitive Advantage.*[8]

- ***Training exclusively in analytic thinking.*** "With respect to the 140,000 MBAs, it is unlikely that even one in a hundred would have been taught anything but inductive and deductive logic during their entire post-secondary education. Many business schools do not merely ignore abductive logic, they inculcate an active hostility to abduction, which is regarded as frivolous. Analytical thinking is presented as not just logically superior but morally superior. That attitude is carried into the workplace."

- *Defending the "proof" of past-based analysis.* "Most executives reached their station in life by studying the past in gruesome detail to chart a course for the future. They have empirical data to support the course they advocate. They are not prepared to evaluate an alternative viewpoint that proceeds not from the basis of what was, but what could be."

How Future-In Strategy Happens

A future-in focus starts from the most important fundamental trends for a company going forward. Each trend is used to challenge the organization's ingrained assumptions, and is assessed on its impact and directly translated into competitive opportunities. This requires two things:

- *Understanding how the relevant trends might affect the company's competitiveness.* For example, we might look at how a change driver affected other sectors or use abductive logic to challenge our thinking with the appropriate what-if questions.

- *Determining the speed of change—today and especially in the future.* For example, which trends represent linear change? Binary change? Step change (such as regulatory mandates)? Or exponential change (such as many high-tech drivers)? How do the fundamental trends influence or interact with one another?

This is not an exact science. It's not like calculating market share, for example. But it is considerably more useful, even if we get it only 80 percent right.

One practical way to capture the results of such efforts is found in what we call a trend impact assessment. Using a 2 × 2 matrix, fundamental trends are plotted on the *x* axis according to their likely importance to the company going forward, and on the *y* axis according to their observed or expected speed of change (see Figure 1.1). In the top right quadrant are the likely sources of true competitive disruption for the company. The bottom right quadrant houses the more predictable but unavoidable competitive developments that must be either capitalized on or safeguarded against. The top left quadrant is home to the fast-changing trends that are deemed less relevant right now, but worth keeping on a watch list in case their relevance shifts over time. Finally, the bottom left quadrant is where we park the less important, slower-moving trends.

Identifying the most important and relevant trends is a chance for the firm's leadership to put its mark on the company's future trajec-

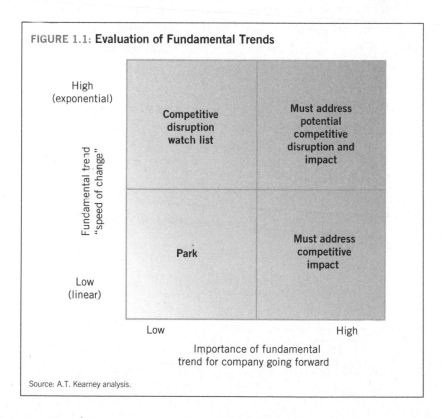

FIGURE 1.1: **Evaluation of Fundamental Trends**

High (exponential)

Competitive disruption watch list

Must address potential competitive disruption and impact

Fundamental trend "speed of change"

Park

Must address competitive impact

Low (linear)

Low   High

Importance of fundamental trend for company going forward

Source: A.T. Kearney analysis.

tory, set the strategic direction, and take the first step toward instilling "mission command" principles, as discussed in the Introduction.

Also, this is the perfect time for inclusiveness. By involving the
broader organization, the firm is able to expand its capacity for abductive logic and bring crucial firsthand experience and tacit knowledge
into the process. It is also a chance to build a broader understanding
of the trends and how they are likely to play out in the near future—
essentially instilling a more anticipatory culture. Even more important,
inclusiveness early on paves the way later when it is time to translate
the trends into discrete competitive opportunities. Each trend becomes
a source of inspiration for what is possible going forward.

An Insurance Firm Looks into the Future

Let's look again at insurance, a sector that was once considered relatively stable. A company in Europe is still conducting business much
as it did in the twentieth century. It is tightly run, efficient, and highly
profitable, but its leaders are concerned that the future of insurance is
likely to be very different from the past.

Drawing on its "foresighting" efforts, scenario planning, and
industry comparisons, the leaders came up with a long list of fundamental trends that are likely to affect the company:

- Digitization of transactional and administrative processes

- Reconfiguration of value chains, dis- and re-intermediation

- Growing peer-to-peer connectivity

- Virtualization of (tacit) knowledge

- Correlation of large data sets

- Eroding social security and benefits

- Aging populations

- Regulatory-enforced transparency

- Deregulation of insurance

- Virtual communities and customer franchises

- Omnichannel distribution

- Crowdsourcing and crowdfunding

The next step is to gain a better understanding of these fundamental trends and their potential impact—either positive or negative—on the company's competitiveness going forward, along with their perceived speed of change. The fundamental trends serve to challenge the organization to think beyond today's situation and consider what might be possible. This allows the leaders to select the trends that they deem most important for the company going forward and outline how the company can take advantage of them. The resulting "strategic game plan" provides the ideal starting point for formulating competitive opportunities.

Once the insurance company had become familiar with the selected trends, it used these trends as inspiration to come up with ideas for creating or increasing the company's competitive advantage. By going through them one by one and asking questions based on abductive logic, each fundamental trend was translated into potential competitive opportunities, which were then distilled and aggregated into discrete competitive opportunities. For example:

Providing end-to-end customer convenience. Customers expect a 24/7 digital environment through which they can manage their affairs—from purchasing insurance coverage to filing claims—cost-effectively and supported by the right tools and applications. The travel industry and online stock trading are good examples of the possibilities.

Providing ubiquitous customer convenience. Customers expect a seamless experience across media and channels that can be tapped whenever and wherever they want.

Offering tailored insurance products to meet customers' real needs. Digital technologies provide the right tools and support so that customers can determine their own coverage needs and configure their own policies. These technologies also make product complexity and configurability both cost-effective and manageable. The automotive, music, and fashion industries are good examples of customers configuring exactly what they want.

Providing financial- and life-planning services (feeding into tailored products). Customers have vast amounts of digital financial, social, life, and health information at their fingertips. Provide the right tools and applications and customers will opt for more tailored products and services.

Leveraging transparency to fuel all-digital and more cost-effective offerings. Both regulatory- and technology-driven transparency make it easier for customers to find and purchase the most attractively priced offerings. While this transparency creates unwanted price erosion for the current business, it provides a future of cost-effective all-digital offerings.

Providing real-time risk coverage and pricing. Mobile technologies and machine-to-machine connectivity make real-time risk coverage and pricing possible, allowing for more competitively priced risk. The success of the pay-as-you-drive and pay-how-you-drive concepts in the United States demonstrates the potential.

Facilitating micromutuality and risk pooling. Technology-fueled social fabric and financial concepts such as peer-to-peer lending and crowdfunding point to the potential for (administering and reinsuring) new microcommunity risk-sharing setups.

In the end, our insurance company did not list regulations such as Solvency II (and Basel III), general economic conditions, aging populations, or prevailing interest rates as being among its most important trends. Despite their obvious profound impact on the company's present situation and immediate future, the leaders decided that these trends were of little direct interest to customers and decided instead to focus on those trends that most influenced the firm's relevance and proposition to customers going forward and deal with these other trends separately. We will leave our insurance company here and pick it up again in later chapters.

Tales of Three Telecoms

The telecom industry has had its fair share of fundamental change over the past few decades: moving from fixed-line to mobile telephony, connecting consumers and businesses to the Internet, dealing with generations of increasingly capable mobile technology, moving from voice to data and from cell phones to smartphones, and 24/7-connected customers. Along the way, the industry has also had to tackle licensing auctions, international expansion, and a wave of mergers, acquisitions, and divestitures.

We have worked with numerous telecoms, helping them deal with everything from their strategic challenges to everyday operational issues. Here, we discuss three companies that approached their strategy formulation in ways that helped them make better sense of the drivers of change that were affecting them and get the decision-making comfort necessary to enable action. Each one faced similar trends, but they had different outcomes.

Telecom 1: Challenge the Prevailing Wisdom

Our first telecom operator is an incumbent player in the Asia-Pacific region with a large domestic market. In the mid-2000s, it faced an array of broad strategic questions, the most significant being (1) whether to expand internationally the way several of its peers in neighboring countries and in Europe had done, (2) how to expand its mobile business after having scaled two mobile networks operating entirely different technologies, and (3) how to deal with adjacent businesses such as information and communications technology (ICT) services and media, which showed tremendous promise for future growth but could also be a distraction.

Telecom 1 wanted help in answering these questions and, importantly, challenging its own leadership and senior management on the drivers of value.

A future-in perspective on the impact of the various fundamental trends indicated that Telecom 1 could expect the value of its traditional business to peak over the next few years, after which the commoditization of mobile voice telephony would take over. The core business would shrink sooner and more profoundly than its leaders had anticipated. The company also concluded that before expanding internationally, it needed to dominate domestic mobile telephony and other domains such as ICT services and select media segments. The company had a relatively large domestic market, and as these market segments intertwined (the result of technology-related trends) and reached critical scale, it would have more to offer internationally.

Telecom 1 formulated a strategy to become the undisputed leader in its home market, doing so against the prevailing wisdom that international expansion should be its top priority. This decision required steadfast conviction. The company faced political pressure to pursue international expansion as its peers had done, with significant pressure coming from within national political parties that were looking for successful examples of the country's globalization policies.

Standing by its decision, the company set up an acquisition and alliance team to grow its presence in domestic ICT services and select media segments. So far, the strategy has been a resounding success. Telecom 1 is now the undisputed market leader domestically across all major segments; has invested in R&D, people development, external partnerships, and innovation; and has taken steps to leverage its position to follow its customers abroad. It has withstood the test of time for more than eight years, surviving three major leadership changes.

Yet, in one instance, management bias crept into the decision-making process. One mobile network that was growing at a double-digit rate was presented as a candidate for divestiture. The facts were compelling, but the network had emotional value to the leaders and the shareholder community, and so the divestiture did not happen. As predicted, the network suffered a decline, and the strategic foresight proved to be right: this business should have been sold when it was still growing. Instead, it eventually wound down and a decade later ceased operations.

Telecom 2: Setting Up a Process

Our second telecom operator is active in another part of the Asia-Pacific region, but one with a much smaller home market. It faced the same mix of aggressive drivers of change, making it obvious that strategic answers would not come from analyzing the company's current position.

Telecom 2 set up an ongoing process to systematically explore the strategic horizon. The company invited strategy consultants, suppliers, and telecom experts to a series of working sessions to share their perspectives on where the industry would be in 2020. With multiple consultants and experts in the same room pitching their views about the future, the team members got a rich outside-in and future-in perspective on their industry. These sessions also gave the team members an opportunity to discuss the implications of a strategy and business model and then synthesize these into their own perspective. The sessions have since become a semiannual retreat to stay in tune with major industry developments (facilitated by the strategy function and owned by all parts of the organization).

From these sessions, the company came to a number of important conclusions:

- Unlike Telecom 1, Telecom 2 would need an international dimension if it was to enjoy meaningful growth.

- Growth would not mean going on an acquisition spree. Rather, the focus would be on new services and business models fueled by technological advances and the necessity of meeting the needs of its increasingly sophisticated customers.

- In terms of its own assets, Telecom 2 would aggressively pursue the possibilities created by an all-IP world, simplifying its setup to give customers innovative products and services and a premium network experience.

Acting on this plan, the company has not only stolen market share from the competition over the past few years but also freed up capital to reinvest in future opportunities. It has also taken a future-in approach to its follow-up efforts. For example, to expand its outsourcing and offshoring, suppliers are invited to collaborate on shaping new services that require a variety of technologies and services to work together in new ways.

Telecom 3: Shared Understanding Through War Gaming

Our third telecom operates predominantly in the Middle East, where players are jockeying for position to capitalize on growth opportunities. Telecom 3 faced the same pressures as many telecom operators across the world: eroding core voice, international voice, and text messaging businesses and data revenue growth; growing customer expectations; blurring telecom boundaries; and technological change.

The company used war gaming to experiment with bold three-year strategies and assess the possible impact of potential competitor moves.[9] The interactive exercise proved effective in getting a cross-functional understanding of how various strategies and trends could play out and evaluating strategic responses. The biggest benefit was that it helped align the leaders and the wider management team on the course of action to take and provided the reassurance needed to act on the insights gained.

The New Strategic Decision Making

The more different the future is likely to be from today, the less convincing a traditional approach to strategy will be. Analyses of the past and extrapolation into the future will fall short in fast-moving and profoundly changing business environments. What's needed is a new form of strategic proof—the kind that comes from a shared understanding of the fundamental drivers of change affecting the company's future, a belief in working together to create winning solutions, and early confirmation of the initiatives that will work.

CHAPTER 2

Organizational Inclusiveness

Tomorrow's business imperatives lie outside the performance envelope of today's bureaucracy-infused management practices.

—GARY HAMEL[1]

IN THE PREVIOUS CHAPTER, we assessed the impact of, and the opportunities created by, the fundamental drivers of change. In this chapter, we look at ways to create a broad strategic understanding throughout the organization, and the most natural transition to making strategy happen.

Hierarchy as an Information Processing System

It's important to understand why a traditional approach of top-down sequential strategy formulation and execution doesn't work in today's fast-changing, dynamic, and increasingly complex business environment.

A century ago, when Frederick Winslow Taylor was developing his theories of scientific management, information and experience were concentrated at the top of the organization. Top management was more educated and had access to more knowledge than the unskilled and often illiterate workers. And in a world where change took place gradually, experience was a huge advantage. Because top managers had more information and more experience, they had decision-making authority and could say with some credibility, "If you knew what I know, you would understand why I made this decision."

Hierarchical bureaucracy was a tool for communicating the direction from the top to the organization below. This worked well enough as long as everything went according to plan. When a problem arose, management got a group of people to work on it. Their proposed solution was consolidated and moved up the chain for approval. The people at the top made the decision.

Then the world changed. Major advances in information and communication technologies, accelerated by the Internet, opened the floodgates so that information flowed both horizontally and vertically. With everyone now having access to the same information, organizational boundaries became porous and the workforce became more educated. In fact, many knowledge workers soon had as much education as—or even more than—their bosses, and employees were often more informed about what was happening "on the ground." In this fast-changing world, years of experience were as likely to be a handicap as an advantage.

So the rationale for concentrating decision making at the top came under scrutiny. People began to work differently, with task forces, project-based plans, process-based teams, and change management initiatives. But the way people worked changed much faster than the way organizations were run. The legacy cultures of hierarchical bureaucracy, sequential processes with approvals up and down the chain, and the structural barriers of organizational silos stayed in place and continued to constrain change. It was hard to dislodge the attitudes, values, and practices of bureaucracy, with its built-in preference for disciplined execution and tight control.

Exercising control through a chain of command was harder than ever. Plans quickly got out of sync as conditions changed. Managers couldn't keep their eyes on everyone and supervise everything. If they tried, they risked being seen as distrustful tyrants who killed creativity and innovation. Yet if they let go of the chain of command, chaos and complexity would overwhelm them.[2]

Fixing Management Is a Precondition for Reclaiming Strategy—and Vice Versa

Companies that want to do something about strategy first have to rethink their management practices. Fortunately, doing something about strategy makes new management practices possible, as strategy changes from a top-down plan that has to be executed into an ongoing guiding framework for organizational inclusiveness in decision making.

Given the obvious advantages when it comes to coping with more dynamic and complex business environments, why aren't more companies moving in this direction? To find the answer, let's consider two management extremes: ultimate bureaucratic managerial control and complete networked freedom.

Traditional bureaucratic management models have reached a point where instructional control is irrelevant. Dynamic, ever-changing business environments require more detailed and more frequent instructions than management can ever provide. What's more, forming effective strategies is nearly impossible, as the amount of information that needs to be gathered and processed is simply too unwieldy. This leaves organizations lacking direction and becoming more reactive.

Networked managerial models transfer decision making to those people in the organization who are on the front lines, and thus are in the best position to gauge the situation and take action. This provides much-needed agility and responsiveness when it comes to dealing with unfolding events. But it doesn't provide *strategic* control. There is no mechanism to ensure that those decentralized decisions are working toward the same goals for the benefit of the whole organization. Popular notions such as customer centricity help create some alignment, but they fall far short of being a proper strategy that generates value for the company.

These are some of the reasons why organizations are reluctant to relinquish traditional bureaucratic and hierarchical forms of control, even though they know that these methods have reached the end of the line. Substituting a model with major but known flaws for another model that is potentially better, but that has a glaring deficiency is not an attractive proposition, especially when facing change management hurdles.

Address Management and Strategy Simultaneously

To overcome the deficiencies in traditional managerial models, management and strategy need to be addressed simultaneously. Networked models have to be introduced alongside a new way of formulating and executing strategy—and this needs to be done in such a way that decentralized decision making and responsiveness can take place within the context of overall strategic guidance.

We will use an example to illustrate this.

A utilities grid company asked us to help with its strategy-driven transformation. Doing so would require resolving several strategic challenges that utilities in the developed world often face and that the company's leaders had identified as priorities within its strategic game plan:

- Transform a central-generation energy system into a decentralized and renewables-based generation network that can accommodate a wide variety of players that both generate and consume power, and at the same time facilitate major changes in government policies without jeopardizing the power supply.

- Accommodate the varied and more detailed workload associated with the new energy system, while defining a value-adding role in the new value chain.

- Make new contributions to and facilitate the management of the resulting energy ecosystem.

And all these things needed to be accomplished while reducing costs and improving performance.

The company also faced a considerable management challenge: large parts of the organization suffered from "transformation fatigue." People lacked enthusiasm for tackling another change: "I'm so tired of all these projects." "Why do they turn everything upside down again and again?" "Shareholders want more money, and we have to take the rap for that." As a result, many of their opinions were not taken into consideration, given the company's history of failed continuous improvement initiatives, and mortality rates for suggestions reached 80 to 90 percent. "We have so many ideas about what should be done, but no one from top management listens to us."[3]

This situation is not unusual. However, reclaiming strategy is impossible if these attitudes persist. A disgruntled and distrustful workforce won't have the energy, attention, or passion required to launch a new strategy. In such settings, the first step is to modify management practices and mobilize the staff members' energy and inspiration.

Strategy from the Middle

The utility also faced a deployment issue. Before the transformation initiative could start, the company had to transform the way thousands of employees worked across more than 100 sites. Management clearly saw the strategic shift that was needed, but it also saw that this could not be accomplished in a classic "blueprint, design, and rollout" fashion. Too much emphasis on the cost side, which invariably affects people, would undermine any willingness on the part of the staff members to explore and develop new capabilities. But going too far in the opposite direction—in a "creative" mode—could make the company even less cost-effective. The challenge was how to achieve the best of both approaches.

The leadership team decided on an approach that is best described as "strategy from the middle," in which top-down strategic guidance is combined with bottom-up mobilization. The idea was to provide strategic direction and guided inspiration while empowering people to find solutions that best fit the challenges that they faced in the field.

Part of this approach involved creating a shadow organization, also called a guiding coalition, to mobilize the middle. People in various management layers (from team leaders on up) assumed part-time roles for the project, with these roles being assigned based on a combination of suitability and self-selection. For example, "strategy navigators" were appointed, coached, and charged with being the driving force for activities. More than 40 strategy navigators became the core of the mobilization, working with part-time colleagues in local action teams. In addition, eight teams of experts focused on interdisciplinary topics.

Overall, more than 1,000 employees (almost 20 percent of the company) were actively involved in determining how to roll out their ideas. This was in clear contrast to conventional top-down programs, where the 15 usual suspects do all the thinking.

Combining Top-Down Guidance with Local Resourcefulness

Strategy navigators, action teams, expert teams, and local staff members got together in local on-the-ground sessions to better understand what would be involved in taking the organization forward. These sessions began not as a top-down communication, but as a dialogue in which inspirations, opportunities, and strategic necessities were reviewed and translated to local situations. This approach provided a mutually reinforcing combination of top-down strategic guidance and local resourcefulness to ensure that the changes and performance improvements could be tackled simultaneously.

Local efforts got considerable support, with strategy navigators and expert teams sharing ideas, best practices, innovations, and strategic solutions from other sessions and industries. One unique practice was the "dogma parking lot." Teams identified ingrained habits and beliefs that were holding the organization back and drove them into a virtual long-term parking lot. Apart from being a source of good-natured fun, it proved liberating to imagine what could be done if the barriers to change were removed.

All in all, the local sessions built up a database of more than 900 practical and executable opportunities. While some of these were fixes for processes and ways of working that were well past their "sell-by" date, others were focused on developing the capabilities required to meet the new strategic requirements. All of them, however, were guided by, and working toward, the strategic direction set by the leadership.

A new sense of energy, a lift in spirits, and a fresh can-do attitude was evident throughout the organization. Without the risk of becoming a victim of forced cost reductions, and with new ways of collaborating, the organization could now take on much more than before.

Building In Network Features

Attitudes, values, and habits cannot be changed overnight. Trust, once lost, takes time to rebuild. Class structures aren't abandoned without a struggle, and much of the old top-down thinking remained embedded in the company's processes and procedures. After the project was "done," the traditional hierarchy and control-focused ways of working gradually returned. The great results were absorbed, but not the new ways of working.

Management was not satisfied with this erosion and set out to correct it by building network features into the hierarchy. It anchored ongoing strategic alignment and hired people with the appropriate skills for new positions with a focus on drawing together and empowering strategy navigators as needed to handle specific opportunities and issues.

The beauty of a more networked management model is that it redefines authority. Leadership in a hierarchy is strongly linked to a person's role, whereas leadership in a networked model is a function of one's demonstrated competencies and capabilities. There is also less need for permanent leadership positions. The needs and opportunities of the moment define the required leadership positions, making networked management models more adaptive and agile.

For most organizations, the transition from authority-based bureaucracy to a fully networked organization is complicated by the fact that there is likely to always be a need for top-down control in some areas. Many companies have parts that need unambiguous, one-directional, stable control and are not necessarily well served by a more dynamic networked management approach. For example, the choice of a networked approach might be clear-cut for a software company developing exciting new applications, but less so for a retail bank with back-office systems that manage millions of customer accounts. We expect our money to be there, and we want to know who is responsible for seeing that it will be. We have similar feelings about safety in refineries and chemical plants, the pilots flying our planes, and other parts of businesses that are well served by control and stability.

Yet banks, airlines, and chemical companies are also operating in more competitive, dynamic, and complex business environments and cannot afford to forfeit the advantages of networked management models. They will have to find a way to reap the benefits of this approach without relinquishing control over the parts of the network that they cannot do without. In such situations, new inclusive approaches to strategy can be a prerequisite for making new forms of management possible.

Organizational Inclusiveness: Why Now?

Bringing the organization into the strategy process is more than a tactic to prompt buy-in. It is a way to incorporate the insights of those who will execute the strategy. Such inclusiveness has several benefits over more traditional top-down strategies:

- It captures firsthand knowledge of what is happening with customers, markets, processes, and technologies. This provides a crucial edge over data analyses and extrapolation.

- It restores a shared sense of purpose, which becomes a source of inspiration and energy and the foundation for the successes ahead.

- It eliminates the handover between those formulating the strategy and those executing it, making it possible to turn strategy from a multiyear sequential process into a continuous guiding framework.

Organizational inclusiveness as a way to bridge gaps between design and execution is not new. There are many well-documented cases and extensive research to show how involving key people helps to improve products, services, processes, and the business. So why is wide-ranging participation rarely considered in strategy formulation? And why should we consider doing so now? In other words, what has changed?

First, there is the practical aspect: we are not making progress in improving the transition from strategy formulation to deployment. In fact, research shows that we might actually be losing ground. This is unacceptable in a world that requires more strategies to be implemented, not fewer.

There are two other factors: we now have new insights about how to motivate knowledge work as opposed to repetitive work, and we have access to the latest collaborative and social technologies that take the reach and richness of collaboration to new levels. Together, these factors make it both necessary and possible to include more people in the strategy process. Let's look at each in more detail.

Motivating Knowledge Work

Extensive research has been done on finding out what inspires and motivates people who perform knowledge work. The results are interesting: the motivational mechanisms for performing mechanical work and routine tasks are profoundly different from those for performing work that requires even modest amounts of cognitive effort. Or as Daniel Pink, the author of *Drive*, puts it: "For routine tasks, which aren't very interesting and don't demand much creative thinking, rewards can provide a small motivational booster shot without the harmful side effects." But Pink observes some significant side effects when it comes to knowledge work: "Money can extinguish intrinsic motivation, diminish performance, crush creativity, encourage unethical behavior, foster short-term thinking, and become addictive."[4]

This, of course, is the opposite of what is needed if we are to craft and implement relevant strategies. Daniel Pink, Dan Ariely, and others who research behavior and motivation have observed that while the nature of work has shifted toward knowledge work, most organizations still rely on monetary incentives that date back to the days of mechanical labor.

Research shows that alternative motivators bring out the best in knowledge workers:

- *Autonomy:* meeting people's desire to direct their own lives and have some say in the outcome

- *Mastery:* putting people in positions where they can fulfill their urge to get better at something that matters

- *Purpose:* allowing people to contribute to a larger, more meaningful cause

This helps explain why traditional top-down approaches to strategy simply don't strike the motivational chords of today's knowledge workers. In a world where more resourcefulness and creativity are needed to bring strategy to life in shorter periods of time, every organization must have the right motivators in place.

The research also helps to explain why, despite the enormous amount of attention it gets, we still cannot claim to have mastered change management. In fact, the opposite is true. When John Kotter researched the effectiveness of change management for his 1996 book *Leading Change*, it turned out to be an abysmal 30 percent. Now, almost two decades later, studies by various parties, including Kotter, show that the success rate is still lingering around the 25 to 30 percent mark. This is not to say that we haven't made progress. After all, our change management challenges have become substantially larger and more complicated. What we can say, however, is that we haven't managed to grow our change management abilities faster than the rate at which our challenges have grown, so we still face extremely unfavorable odds.

Beyond personal motivation, research into organizational motivation provides another explanation for the inability to master change management.

The very need for change management suggests that there is a solution that has to be implemented, and to do so, we need to get people to think differently about what they are doing and to adapt their behavior accordingly. From the outset, this appears to be at odds with the three motivators—autonomy, mastery, and purpose—that bring out the best in people. It puts change management at a disadvantage as organizations come to be driven more by knowledge work and strategies become more complex and numerous. But research also suggests a way out of this conundrum. Pink observes: "Questions are often more effective than statements in moving others. Or to put it more appropriately, since the research shows that when the facts are on your side, questions are more persuasive than statements, don't you think you should be pitching more with questions?" This helps to explain why the questions raised in abductive logic are so effective— they simultaneously engage the organization and help to resolve the right challenges.

Reconsidering the combination of strategy formulation and change management in the light of autonomy, mastery, and purpose reveals a distinct upside to formulating strategy in an organizationally broad manner: it effectively reduces, and can even eliminate, the need for change management and checks all the motivational boxes at the same time.

An organization that is involved in strategy formulation has influence over the outcome, fosters employees' understanding and contributions, and strengthens an organizational sense of purpose. Bringing people into the dialogue can be a powerful motivator, as Kotter observes in his *Harvard Business Review* article "Accelerate!" Organizations can readily motivate people to participate in coalitions of the willing that drive the company's strategic frontiers, Kotter states.

We believe that this type of inclusiveness offers the best of both worlds: independent initiatives secure the future of the organization while drawing on the best that the organization has to offer. This willingness to participate is strong enough to induce individuals to make this contribution on top of their daily responsibilities. Although the latter is not a sustainable solution, it does show the power of autonomy, mastery, and purpose as organizational motivators.

Technological Advancement

The latest technological advances can take organizational inclusiveness to new levels by allowing for almost frictionless participation across departments, functions, business units, hierarchies, geographies, and even time. Collaborative and social tools are especially well suited for escaping the constrictions of in-person meetings and improving interactions with far more people.

Most companies have rolled out the best known of these tools, such as SharePoint, Yammer, Google Business Apps, Basecamp, Jive, Podio, and others. (This list does not begin to cover the vast number of tools available.) While many companies confess that they do not use these collaborative tools as much as they should—continuing to rely heavily on communicating via email, for example—the tools are usually available and ready for new uses such as organization-wide strategy formulation.

IBM has been pioneering collaborative innovation since 2001 with Jam, its massive online conferencing tool. First used to answer questions such as how to get IBM consulting into boardrooms, IBM took Jam further in 2006 by using it for innovation. In a multiday session, more than 150,000 people from organizations across more than 100 countries shared new and innovative ideas. Yet, while the session demonstrated Jam's effectiveness in bringing together a staggering number of ideas, the conversations did not immediately coalesce into shared visions. These emerged afterward from going through tens of thousands of ideas and comments. Since then, a great deal has been learned on how to refine the balance between the breadth of ideation and the focus required to get to shared visions.

Putting Tacit Knowledge to Use

Strategy formulation in an organizationally involved setting is unique. Rather than using analyses and information to determine which fundamental trends will have the biggest impact on the company—positive and negative—the strategy team draws on the collective knowledge and expertise of the organization.

Doing so requires a different mindset and an understanding of how to tap into tacit knowledge and expertise. Unlike explicit knowledge, tacit knowledge resides in employees' heads in the form of expertise, experience, judgment, creativity, and imagination. Such knowledge cannot be readily captured and reused. The only good way to access it is not to capture it, but simply to put it to use. In practical terms, this means letting the organization work on issues for which it needs this tacit knowledge. This is why structured workshops and face-to-face settings are so effective in coming up with solutions. However, they are not very scalable, and considerable effort is often required to disseminate their output, which limits their effectiveness.

This is where collaborative and social technologies come into play. These tools allow for interaction with a richness approaching that of physical settings. Add to this almost unlimited scalability and new opportunities to draw on a group's collective tacit knowledge, archive the output, and provide measurability, and these technologies become an almost perfect complement to face-to-face interactions (see the sidebar "Unleashing Organizational Brain Power" on page 54).

Collaborative and social tools also lend themselves to more intricate and nuanced applications. Consider a workshop where a multidisciplinary, international group of 100 people are meeting to find ways to take advantage of a new business opportunity, evaluate the usefulness and feasibility of their ideas, assess the implications, and determine the immediate priorities. A virtual equivalent of such a workshop has many advantages, from the obvious (no need to find a date and venue, absorb travel costs, or facilitate a constructive dialogue) to the less obvious (a virtual workshop can be spread over several weeks to allow people to participate when it suits them from wherever they are).

Most organizations have used technology-enabled ideation or crowdsourcing in one way or another. But there are many more techniques, which can be grouped into four types: gather, substantiate, evaluate, and synthesize (see Figure 2.1).

Of course, studies about using technology to enable organizational inclusiveness observe that the synthesis and convergence of ideas does not happen automatically. As MIT's Osvald Bjelland and Robert Chapman Wood observe in their article "An Inside View of IBM's Innovation Jam":[5]

> Ideas didn't bubble up and get refined through continual, respectful dialogue. In fact, few contributors built constructively on each other's postings. The Innovation Jam was organized to capture a huge number of ideas from IBM's network, and it was purposely designed not to guide conversation artificially toward a quick focus on a few thoughts. But without organizers pushing toward an artificial consensus, conversations did not move toward consensus by themselves. Rather than emerging during the online conversations, new visions emerged afterward. IBM had developed a carefully thought-out process that it used after each phase of the Jam to harvest ideas.

Our experience with strategy projects is similar. But rather than following a sequential approach, we try to merge or overlap the stages

FIGURE 2.1: Four Types of Technology-Enabled Inclusiveness

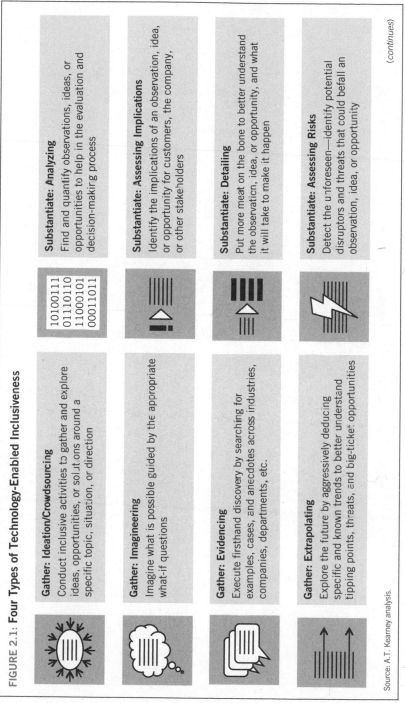

Gather: Ideation/Crowdsourcing
Conduct inclusive activities to gather and explore ideas, opportunities, or solutions around a specific topic, situation, or direction

Substantiate: Analyzing
Find and quantify observations, ideas, or opportunities to help in the evaluation and decision-making process

Gather: Imagineering
Imagine what is possible guided by the appropriate what-if questions

Substantiate: Assessing Implications
Identify the implications of an observation, idea, or opportunity for customers, the company, or other stakeholders

Gather: Evidencing
Execute firsthand discovery by searching for examples, cases, and anecdotes across industries, companies, departments, etc.

Substantiate: Detailing
Put more meat on the bone to better understand the observation, idea, or opportunity, and what it will take to make it happen

Gather: Extrapolating
Explore the future by aggressively deducing specific and known trends to better understand tipping points, threats, and big-ticket opportunities

Substantiate: Assessing Risks
Detect the unforeseen—identify potential disruptors and threats that could befall an observation, idea, or opportunity

(continues)

Source: A.T. Kearney analysis.

FIGURE 2.1: Four Types of Technology-Enabled Inclusiveness *(continued)*

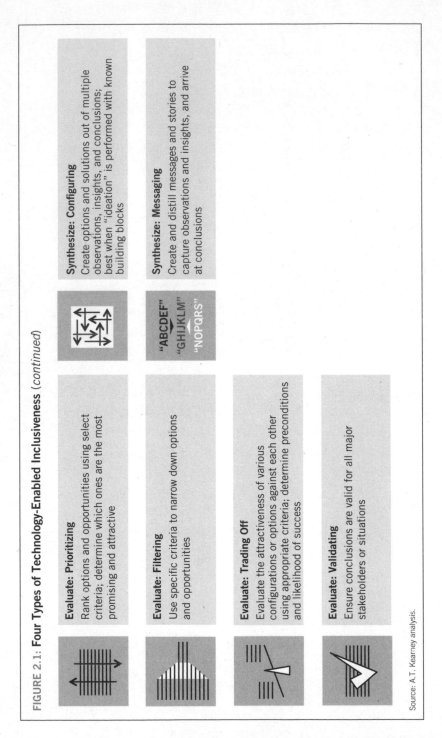

Evaluate: Prioritizing
Rank options and opportunities using select criteria; determine which ones are the most promising and attractive

Evaluate: Filtering
Use specific criteria to narrow down options and opportunities

Evaluate: Trading Off
Evaluate the attractiveness of various configurations or options against each other using appropriate criteria; determine preconditions and likelihood of success

Evaluate: Validating
Ensure conclusions are valid for all major stakeholders or situations

Synthesize: Configuring
Create options and solutions out of multiple observations, insights, and conclusions; best when "ideation" is performed with known building blocks

Synthesize: Messaging
Create and distill messages and stories to capture observations and insights, and arrive at conclusions

Source: A.T. Kearney analysis.

as much as possible. Going back to our example, the core team—made up of 40 strategy navigators—sees itself not as the main synthesizer and idea-converging force in the effort, but as the guide on the strategic journey.

As the organizer, the core team is in charge of the journey's itinerary. The team brings the chosen fundamental trends to life with facts, figures, examples, and stories and challenges the group by asking the appropriate questions in a constructive sequence. This deploys the organization's collective strength toward synthesis and the convergence of ideas. Generally, the core team works harder at synthesis and convergence than it does at gathering intelligence or ideation.

The online suggestion box can help us illustrate this. We all know about suggestion boxes on the company intranet, and we also know that these boxes are not always effective. An executive we spoke with summarized the problem quite harshly: "All we get through the suggestion box are complaints and a bunch of wild suggestions that we can't follow up on in a million years." But when asked how often he used the suggestion box to ask for help with a specific issue or opportunity, he admitted that he had never even visited it. We challenged him to send an email with a question about an important issue he was dealing with to a substantial part of his organization across hierarchies. He would ask for suggestions and add a link to the suggestion box for replies and discussion. After some thought, he sent out the following email to the entire sales and marketing department:

> We are very happy when we land new customers. It is proof that our strategy is working and that we can add value to our customers' lives and that they chose us over our competitors. Today, however, we are not really telling our customers that we are happy that we have won their business. How can we let our customers know in a practical and affordable way that we are delighted to have the opportunity to serve them?

This time around, the suggestion box had a lot of focused activity and some very useful suggestions (as well as some pretty exotic ones).

The executive visited the suggestion box and asked several follow-up and clarifying questions, which sparked further discussion. In the end, several useful ideas emerged, two of which were implemented. Apart from the practical aspects of using the suggestion box, the executive also realized that the way he asked the question helped him share some of the values that he felt were important for the business.

UNLEASHING ORGANIZATIONAL BRAIN POWER

A few years ago, we had a conversation with the head of a European specialty additives division. We'll call her Ms. T. The company is well known—actually famous—in certain circles for selling tailored products that are geared toward meeting every customer's explicit needs.

Ms. T was not in the best of moods that day. Her division was dealing with problems that at the time seemed overwhelming. She told us about the difficulty she was having in finding product specialists who had the knowledge—or at least the right kind of knowledge—to help customers apply the division's products.

"Yes, we as a company are great at developing specialty products, each one designed to meet a customer's individual needs," she said. "And our product specialists are smart—we have some of the brightest minds in the industry, in fact. These specialists know our products inside and out, and yet, despite this, our overall support is failing."

We had to leave the conversation there, as both she and we had to rush off to our meetings.

A few weeks later, we ran into Ms. T again in Paris. She was there to interview two more product specialists, but one of the interviews had been postponed. As management consultants, we were not about to let this opportunity get away. Instead of a quick meet and greet in the hallway, we asked her to join us for lunch. It didn't take long before we were deep in conversation about the inherent problems of selling and supporting specialty products.

"It's not so much a challenge to find sufficient knowledge inside the firm," she explained. "After all, throughout our organizations in Europe, we have more than 70 specialists. And between them, at least in principle, they can resolve any issue with any customer, no matter how difficult."

The longer we talked, the clearer things became. The problems seemed to be most prevalent at the country level. It was difficult to provide the right level and mix of expertise necessary to deal with each and every customer issue in each and every country.

We had an idea for a new approach. We asked her to take a page from our book (yes, this one) and approach two or three of her most seasoned product specialists. "Choose carefully," we said, "because these people have to have proved their mettle within the company and must be respected by their peers."

We scratched out the plan on a napkin: The next time there is a real challenge—a tough, difficult-to-solve problem for an important client—ask the assigned specialist to post the problem on a private workspace on the company's intranet. (This might take some convincing, since specialists are not prone to avoid challenges.) Then, have the specialist send an email to all 70 product specialists with a question: "Can anyone help us come up with a 'wow' solution to this client's problem? The kind of solution that will win us more business with this important client?" Remind the specialist to include within the message a link to the private workspace to capture the answers and suggestions.

Charles M. in Germany was the first to take on the challenge. He said he was pleasantly surprised as the solutions poured in, mostly from specialists in other countries who had solved a similar problem for their clients. "And," Charles admitted, "a couple of the solutions were better than what I would have come up with on my own." It didn't take long before other specialists were making use of the workspace to post some of their more challenging requests.

Since then, the dynamics have been getting even more interesting. The company's workspace is growing larger and becoming a more valuable resource, as all requests and answers are searchable. This not only gives the specialists access to a growing amount of captured collective knowledge, but also helps them identify people with particular knowledge—what Ms. T began calling her specialists' specialties. Before long, human resources personnel were involved. They followed the posts, both problems and solutions, in order to make sure that those who contributed the most to the firm's success were properly rewarded.

This is just one of many examples that illustrate the value of organizational inclusiveness. Yet, even as many organizations are beginning to use collaborative and social tools to capture the best thinking and ideas within their organizations, there are generally more disappointments than there are successes. That's because there can be a stiff learning curve for unlocking the collective knowledge of an organization.

What separates Ms. T's experience from that of less successful firms? We asked her that question. She thinks it has to do with the people in her division. "Our specialists are willing to put aside their egos if they can serve their clients better," she explained. "No one feels the need to keep the biggest, most challenging problems to themselves so that they can swoop in and 'save the day.' Everyone does what is best for the company as a whole."

Then she paused, obviously rethinking this: "Maybe it's more personal than that. Maybe we got better at including more people because it made all of our lives easier, because we are able to deliver better solutions to our customers with less effort. What's not to like about that?"

Leadership: Creating an Inspirational Journey

Organizational inclusiveness is not only about collaborative and social tools. Success hinges on having a leadership team that is able to translate project objectives into an inspirational journey that challenges current mindsets.

An inspiring journey can be configured in question and interaction (Q&I) cycles. It begins with a challenging question (or task) that is brought to life with the appropriate supporting materials. Each cycle has a predefined desired output—an insight, conclusion, ranking, risk assessment, or plan. This avoids open dialogue that leads to too many ideas and not enough follow-through.

The central component of a Q&I cycle is the different forms of interaction. Q&I cycles are essentially evolving mini-journeys, with multiple subquestions and intermediate steps needed to achieve the overall desired output.

In the early stages, the leadership and the project team typically want to test their choice of guiding direction. The request to the group might be: "Our scenario-planning exercise has identified five fundamental trends as the most important for us out of more than 25 trends. We need to validate this selection." For each of the five trends, the group provides examples, figures, and other material that explain what this fundamental trend is and why it is important. The group can also organize events, workshops, and webinars to bring the trends to life (or leave this for later when it explores the implications of these trends and the competitive opportunities resulting from them).

In terms of output, the group might rank the trends according to their perceived speed of change and their likely importance to the company going forward. This often requires breaking down the main question or task into subdialogues that explore parts of the challenge. For example:

- Are there important fundamental trends that are missing from the selection?

- Are there trends in the selection that should not be included?

- How should the trends be ranked to determine their relative importance and speed of change? How much more powerful will the trends be in five years?

- Which trends will be most influential in determining whether or not we are successful in the future?

- How should the trends be ranked in terms of our ability to take advantage of them?

- Which trends provide us with an opportunity because of our culture, DNA, capabilities, or market position compared to those of the competition?

To answer such questions, the group might use discussion forums, polls, and mini-surveys, which are likely to lead to follow-up questions that can be addressed along the way.

A strategy formulation journey typically has multiple nested Q&I cycles that work together to create the desired output. So the journey must be flexible enough to accommodate a particular strategic challenge or company situation.

How Not to Lose Control

Organizational inclusiveness, especially when pursued with some ambition, requires taking precautions to avoid a loss of control. There are several ways to maintain levels of strategic control beyond what can be achieved through top-down approaches.

Before discussing these, it is important to remember that organizational inclusiveness is not suitable for every strategic challenge. There will always be situations that require traditional top-down strategy development—for example, those that demand confidentiality, such as M&A strategies and due diligence efforts, and turnaround and restructuring situations in which tough decisions must be made about the workforce.

Instill Trust, Be Sincere

The foundation of organizational inclusiveness is creating trust and mutual understanding. Trust must permeate up and down the chain of command and across business units. Like respect, it must be earned. It is reciprocal in nature: managers must trust their subordinates, and subordinates must trust their managers. Subordinates are more likely to take on a project when their managers trust them. They will also be more willing to encourage inventiveness among their own subordinates if they trust that their manager will accept and support the outcome.[6]

There are no shortcuts to gaining trust. While it is often gained slowly, trust can be lost quickly when mistakes are made under pressure or statements reveal hidden intent. Saying one thing and doing something else is another quick way to lose trust.

Bringing in people from throughout the organization can be a great contributor to deepening trust, but it cannot fix a lack of trust. It also cannot be used for objectives that are bound to erode trust. As mentioned earlier, figuring out how to lay off 20 percent of the workforce is not a strategic challenge that lends itself to organizational inclusiveness.

The biggest prerequisite is being genuinely all-encompassing so that the organization becomes a core part of the strategy formulation process. If you involve people only as a tactic to increase their potential buy-in for preconceived strategies, this will invariably backfire and cause or add to the distrust. People cannot be fooled about this, so the decision to involve the organization in strategy formulation requires commitment. Once this involvement has started, it cannot be stopped without triggering distrust and making it much harder to attempt involvement again.

Avoid the Seemingly Endless "Ideation" Tangle

Controls are necessary to prevent inclusiveness from turning into a wildly divergent ideation event. Keeping everyone on track requires the use of fundamental trends and strategic game plans as inspiration to guide the strategy efforts. Leaders use these to set the direction for strategy development. Selecting fundamental trends obviously provides a clear overall direction. But their sequencing in the strategic journey and the challenging questions put to the organization also help to guide the development efforts. This allows the leaders to accommodate the most important trade-offs at the corporate level and to influence control over the targeted output of the strategy.

Choose the Appropriate Travel Party

Another major source of control comes from the design of the journey. Its depth, breadth, and density can be tailored to the strategic situation at hand. There are several overriding requirements for every strategic journey:

- *Self-selection.* Those included have to be at least partly self-selected. From a motivational perspective, people need some autonomy in deciding whether or not to participate. This also helps tilt the balance toward participants who are enthusiastic and willing to engage and away from those who simply feel obligated to do so. Appointing the usual suspects—trusted by the leadership—is counterproductive.

- *Overcapacity.* To ensure sufficient capacity and power to resolve issues, it is always better to be somewhat overly inclusive rather than trying to get by with too few people; the latter will not create the multidisciplinary critical mass necessary to resolve issues and formulate attractive competitive opportunities. We often think in terms of three dimensions, each with a specific use (see Figure 2.2):

   Depth. The people you include can range from the leadership team and a core project group all the way down to frontline employees. Long-term, game-changing, explorative strategies usually require a smaller group of key people with deep knowledge and experience.

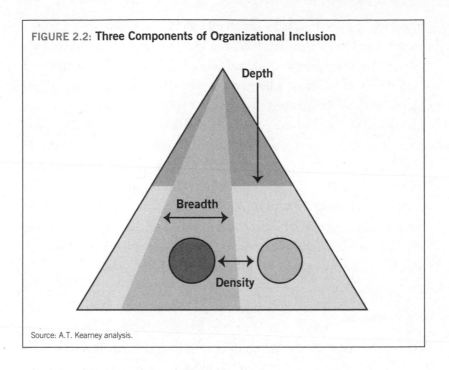

FIGURE 2.2: **Three Components of Organizational Inclusion**

Depth

Breadth

Density

Source: A.T. Kearney analysis.

Breadth. Inclusiveness can reach across all functions, business units, and geographies or focus more narrowly on a specific domain. Even when the topic requires focused participation, cross-functional participation can help forge truly integral strategies.

Density. Including everyone across the board is best for near-term, performance-focused efforts that require high levels of mobilization. The need for significant cultural or behavioral change can also be a reason to aim for broader, deeper, and especially more dense participation. Of course, inclusion requires some thought, as there is a wide spectrum of choices, from appointing key people to inviting absolutely everyone.

As an example, we worked with a high-tech company to revisit its strategy in the light of a postmerger integration. The company opted for *open inclusion*, in which all 60,000 old and new employees were invited to a three-day Jam to help translate six strategic planks into the necessary organizational behaviors. Hosted by 200 trained facilitators, more than 8,000 employees contributed to the effort, offering ideas for strategic opportunities, commenting on other ideas, and evaluating the outcomes. At the other end of the spectrum is *appointed inclusion*. We helped a brewing company subsidiary get consensus and acceptance from 40 key people in an intense one-month strategy formulation effort. There's also an in-between approach, *leveraged inclusion*, in which a cross section of trusted people is invited to participate, and a cascaded invitation process is triggered as they invite other people who invite still others. Table 2.1 highlights the pros and cons of each approach.

Be Transparent

One of the most important sources of strategic control is transparency. The entire strategy process has to be a "no-secrets-here" zone in which everyone contributes to the process and everyone sees all the contributions.

There is no substitute for transparency. It is a champion for trusting people with information, and the antithesis to backroom politics and deal making. Transparency in formulating strategy captures the richness of the interactions and turns them into a searchable repository of dialogues and reasoning for future reference. Over time, transparency even creates a unique sort of yellow pages of the organization's skills and competencies, for example, using keywords to search for individuals who contributed to the strategic dialogue.

Perhaps most important, transparency can form the basis for performance management approaches that are better suited to networked organizations. People who contribute to the strategy formulation efforts—especially those who do so in addition to their regular duties—can be recognized for their contributions based on the trails they leave.

TABLE 2.1

Appointed Inclusion	Leveraged Inclusion	Open Inclusion
Select people, typically chosen by leadership and management teams or through hierarchical invitations such as the top 200, are invited to the strategy effort.	Cascading and networked invitations are given to people, along with invitations to pass on to others—people who they believe can make valuable contributions or who have expressed interest.	Open invitations are extended to large parts of the organization.
Pros:	**Pros:**	**Pros:**
Provides a measure of (perceived) control	Creates a sense of ownership and responsibility for contributing	Ensures substantial capacity and representation
Allows for balanced representation of businesses, functions, and geographies (or a deliberate focus)	Brings about a bias toward enthusiastic and contributing people	Is suitable for organizational mobilization in the event that the strategy is well known up front
	Offers an effective way to create scalable inclusion	
Cons:	**Cons:**	**Cons:**
Not all appointed members are equally enthusiastic or opportunity-focused	Not suitable for broad mobilization	Not suitable for sensitive competitive opportunities or longer-term explorative strategy formulation
Feelings of representation can restrict freedom of contributing	Might need significant scale to achieve the desired representation or to actively manage the required contributions	Forces compromises in the setup of an inclusive journey to accommodate large numbers of people, often limiting interaction to events and interventions instead of having an ongoing dialogue
Can be cumbersome to organize for larger strategies and may not be suitable for mobilization	Requires follow-up for recognition of valuable contributions (HR)	Risk of distraction by organization-wide issues
Does not convey a spirit of being all-encompassing		
Can stifle constructive dialogue		

Consider the Human Implications

Organizational inclusiveness in strategy, especially in its early incarnations, is often "volunteer work" in the sense that it thrives on passion and excitement. However, strategy formulation shouldn't be either something that participants do on their personal time or something that they do during working hours that results in their "regular work" being pushed to evenings and weekends. Formulating strategy *is* part of people's regular work and needs to be budgeted as such.

Here again, collaborative and social tools become vital components, both to capture the richness of the strategic interactions and to provide information about individuals' contributions so that they can be duly recognized. Ongoing recognition is especially important to ensure that strategic management is not seen as a temporary initiative that will come to an end after a burst of activity, causing the organization to revert to its hierarchical bureaucracy and business as usual.

What If Everybody Knows My Strategy?

When discussing organizational inclusiveness with executives, a popular question is, "If our entire organization helps formulate our strategy, won't the entire world know it as well, and won't that undermine our ability to create competitive advantage?" This is a valid question, and there are two parts to the answer.

Other companies or people *knowing* about your strategy will not be an issue as long as you are *doing* your strategy faster and better than others. If your strategy is a secret, however, and your organization doesn't even know about it, you cannot expect the organization to execute it swiftly. So if you are going to share your strategy with your organization, you might as well do it in such a way that it optimally contributes to strategy deployment. In other words, invite the organization into the formulation process. After all, keeping your strategy a secret will frustrate the deployment of it so much that it had better be kept a secret.

Organizational Inclusiveness Is a Bargain

We do not want to leave the impression that organizational inclusiveness, if done properly, is a lot of work. It's not. On the contrary, including more people in strategy formulation can save considerable amounts of time and work down the road. Consider what typical sequential and cascading strategy efforts look like. These ivory tower strategy teams figure out things that the organization already knows, while the formulated strategies face "not invented here syndrome" and considerable change management hurdles. And when, or if, the strategy is finally implemented, there are usually design flaws that compromise its effectiveness. But the strategy would have been compromised anyway because it takes too long to implement. Imagine all of this *and* the typical 30 percent change management success rate. Clearly, compared to the workload of dealing with and correcting a typical strategy process, the extra effort required to include the organization in the process looks like a bargain.

MARKETING TAKES A NEW APPROACH

After the fall of Lehman Brothers and the start of the global economic and financial crisis, an international banking division needed a new global marketing strategy. It was clear that its pre-crisis positioning and marketing approach would no longer cut it and might even be counterproductive given the degree to which the general public blamed the banking sector for the crisis.

Traditionally, the bank would have pulled together a project team, set up a steering committee, created a new global marketing strategy, and rolled out that strategy across all regions and countries. This time, given the sensitivities and the need to act swiftly, the bank pursued a more organizationally involved approach.

The project team started by inviting the global marketing community to a virtual meeting, hosted on its internal collaborative platform. The team explained the details and then asked the marketers a series of questions in two-week cycles. Answers were collected on the collaborative platform for everybody to see and comment on.

In the first cycle, everyone was asked to share the marketing efforts that had been effective in his or her country and to discuss the ones that he or she believed would be useful going forward. Each country wanted to share its successes, of course, so the repository of compelling marketing ideas grew. The team also asked which competitor initiatives had been effective and could serve as inspiration for the bank's own global marketing strategy. The team then took a step back and identified the main themes running through the examples.

In the next cycle, the marketing community was asked to evaluate various trade-offs among the themes to reveal what the priorities should be. By asking the entire community, the team was able to identify which themes had regional biases that should be accommodated in the marketing strategy.

Based on the main themes and the trade-offs, the project team drafted a strategy and presented it to the marketing community. The marketers were asked for feedback not only about how to make the strategy better, but also about aspects of the strategy that would not work in specific countries or regions and how to resolve these issues in a practical way. After incorporating the feedback, the team sought formal approval from the steering committee (which had been kept up to date during the entire process) and cycled the strategy back to the community.

During the last cycle, the team focused on the necessary actions to roll out the marketing strategy by asking each country to submit an action plan in a format that allowed rolling all the countries' efforts into a single plan that could be monitored for progress.

This simplified example shows several major differences from traditional strategy formulation projects. First, formulation and execution blur to form a single continuous journey. Because the entire marketing community is involved in formulating the strategy, ownership of the results is shared with the organization from day one. This makes strategy projects in an involved setting somewhat binding, for there is no easy way back if the leaders decide to adopt a different course.

CHAPTER 3

Managing the Competitive Portfolio

Any leadership position is transitory and likely to be short-lived.

—Peter Drucker[1]

Strategy is an organization's clear and guiding source of energy, fueling the creation of excited customers who are happy to part with their money in order to receive certain goods and services.

But according to a 2013 A.T. Kearney study, strategy is facing conflicting challenges.[2] On the one hand, companies are under pressure to deal with the short term: 63 percent of executives and strategy professionals say that their strategy cycle is now two years or less, and 42 percent say that it is getting even shorter. One-third believe that agility is now the cornerstone of strategy, and half say that a combination of strategy and agility is required. Only 19 percent believe that the pursuit of competitive advantage *is still* the main goal of their strategy.

The study also reveals that 85 percent of companies with a strategic horizon of five years or more consider their strategies to be effective, compared with less than half for those with shorter cycles.

These findings should not be surprising to anyone. Fast-changing, increasingly dynamic business environments are forcing companies to react and adapt in the here and now while also making more profound, complex choices concerning the future. If the answer lies in strategy—and we believe it does—then strategy has to bridge the gap between being a periodically formulated overall direction and becoming a continuous guiding force.

The military principles of "mission command," discussed in the Introduction, provide inspiration for how strategy can bridge the gap. Strategy formulation and execution is an ongoing activity, not a sequential concept. In war, a portfolio of missions is maintained based on conditions on the ground, lessons learned during the missions, and periodic recalibration of the overall strategic direction. In business, the equivalent of mission command is a portfolio of competitive opportunities that is maintained based on the fundamental trends affecting the business, feedback from the initiatives executed in pursuit of these competitive opportunities, and the periodic recalibration of overall strategic direction.

We use the word *opportunity* because, as with a military mission, there is always competitive advantage to be achieved—even if the opportunity is already contributing to the success of the company.

What Are Competitive Opportunities and How Are They Used?

In Chapter 1, we discussed how to identify competitive opportunities by asking questions that are based on abductive logic and inspired by the most important trends affecting the company going forward. In principle, competitive opportunities include anything that contributes to creating value for customers, delivering that value, and capturing at least some of that value as a reward. These are essential components of a new way of managing strategy. In Chapter 2, we explained that reclaiming strategy entails managing differently—shifting from issuing detailed instructions from the top to involving the entire organization in strategy formulation and execution. In this chapter, we discuss continually adapting the portfolio of competitive opportunities to guide actions throughout the organization.

FutureProof strategy plays out on three levels:

- *Define the strategic game plan.* The game plan articulates the why of the business—essentially, the purpose of the organization. It is the basis for choosing which competitive opportunities to pursue and which ones to discard because they are not central to the firm's future.

- *Manage the competitive opportunities.* A set of discrete potential sources of competitive advantage that are at various stages in their respective life cycles is chosen and maintained. The selection is based on the game plan to ensure cohesiveness and that the designated opportunities are mutually reinforcing.

- *Execute the initiatives.* Implementation involves executing a set of initiatives in pursuit of the competitive opportunities. The idea is not to add new initiatives to ongoing activities (putting an even heavier burden on the organization), but to evaluate all ongoing initiatives to determine which ones are aligned with the firm's competitive opportunities, which ones are counterproductive, and what new initiatives are needed (see Figure 3.1).

FIGURE 3.1: **From Two to Three Strategic Levels**

Traditional Strategy

Develop a strategy

Strategic initiatives

"Mission Command" Strategy

Define a strategic game plan (direction)

Manage a portfolio of competitive opportunities (goals)

Executive strategic initiatives (action)

Source: A.T. Kearney analysis.

Dealing with Three Time Horizons

The three levels in FutureProof strategy provide short-, medium-, and long-term coverage.

The strategic game plan provides long-term continuity. It brings together the fundamental trends that the firm wants to take advantage of, the logic and boundaries it plans to use, and indirectly its culture and values to provide grounding and stability. The game plan is far more specific than the mission or vision statement. It embodies the overall logic of where the firm is heading and how it is going to win in the marketplace.

The competitive opportunities sit between the long-term horizon of the game plan and the hectic dynamic of executing initiatives on a daily basis. They provide clear competitive goals to aim for while acknowledging that these goals are not permanent—they have a life cycle. By managing the life cycles of competitive opportunities, the firm achieves a balance between dealing with today's realities and anticipating the future.

The initiatives are the here and now of strategy, as they embody the actions needed to capitalize on the competitive opportunities. As each initiative is developed and implemented, the organization can experiment with and reevaluate the competitive opportunities. Initiatives signal when the portfolio requires a shift, and are adapted as circumstances on the ground change. Because competitive opportunities are continually managed as a portfolio, new insights can be incorporated quickly into all affected initiatives.

From a Bunch of Initiatives to a Portfolio of Competitive Opportunities

Companies often try to implement strategy by using a program of initiatives, based on a plan that sets the overall milestones and objectives.

The difficulties with this approach begin when things don't go according to plan. Developments in the marketplace—a new product, a new technology, or a shift in customer preferences—can abruptly undermine the company's competitive position and require giving urgent attention to multiple initiatives.

This is where things get complicated because of the many interrelationships among the various initiatives. It's important for the firm to move quickly to either capture an advantage or stem the losses. Yet giving urgent attention can be cumbersome, as it requires reevaluating the relevant initiatives and their interrelationships. So, too often, rather than addressing the market development, the firm muddles through with unaligned and inconsistent initiatives until the next planning cycle.

With our approach, initiatives are taken from a portfolio of competitive opportunities. In the event of an abrupt market change, the organization has a keen understanding of the explicit and managed interrelationships among the opportunities and the implications of these interrelationships. A response can be formulated quickly and effectively.

Another difficulty with managing strategy at the initiative level is that, given the increasing scale and complexity of business, it becomes too difficult for the leaders to provide detailed instructions for all the initiatives. This tends to leave the task of direction setting to individual project teams—which often means duplication of effort, misaligned goals, and missed synergies between initiatives. For example, it is not unusual to have inconsistent initiatives, with some aiming to cut costs and others seeking to add customer value by drawing on the same capabilities that are being subjected to cost cutting.

Acknowledging the Life Cycle of Competitive Opportunities

One important advantage of maintaining a portfolio of competitive opportunities is that their life cycles can be managed; the firm can pursue emerging opportunities while disengaging from fading opportunities. This sounds straightforward, but it is of great significance for managing strategy.

Companies that face more issues and opportunities than they can handle have to set priorities. Setting priorities at the level of strategic initiatives invariably leads to a bias toward taking care of the most urgent and pressing short-term issues at the expense of longer-term opportunities. In other words, the company takes out a mortgage on its future to fix a leaky roof.

By comparison, when the company is armed with a coherent portfolio of competitive opportunities and a strategic game plan, initiatives can be prioritized based on a balanced reference point. Thus, even a housekeeping initiative, such as a necessary upgrading of the IT platform, can help lay the foundation for tomorrow's new capability of technology-enabled customer service.

A portfolio approach is also conducive to organizational inclusiveness. When there are people throughout the organization who understand both the strategic game plan and the competitive opportunities that fit within that plan, there are many eyes and ears that are able to spot new opportunities and threats, make adjustments on the fly, and cull fading opportunities—without waiting for instructions from above.

Sizing Up Competitive Opportunities

While fundamental trends can be translated into discrete competitive opportunities, turning these opportunities into a coherent portfolio requires properly sizing them up.

It would be nice if competitive advantage could be easily calculated, but this is often not possible, since advantage can originate from a variety of sources. For example, it can come from a specific capability or positioning, an innovative product or service, a patent, a unique way of serving customers, or the ability to do something faster, better, or cheaper than the competition. Competitive advantage can also be found in hiring strategies (see the sidebar "Take the Essential Next Step in Your Career").

Competitive opportunities can be defined in terms of "where to play," "how to win," or a combination thereof. The focus is determined by market conditions, the specific characteristics of the company and its situation, and its leaders' decisions about where and how to compete and which fundamental trends to pursue.

Competitive opportunities will often be interdependent and mutually reinforcing. Also, they are increasingly interrelated, encompassing entire ecosystems aimed at truly delighting customers—not once but on an ongoing basis. For example, going back to our insurance company, we might define several interrelated competitive opportunities:

- Offer virtual self-help advice that allows consumers to figure out their own risk mitigation needs.

- Develop self-configurable products so that consumers can take out exactly the coverage they need for the right price.

- Provide a digitized process that gives consumers control in a cost-competitive way.

Competitive opportunities imply a promise of sustained advantage and are therefore crucial components of a strategy that anticipates the future. This doesn't mean that competitive opportunities are all "greenfield." On the contrary, established businesses are likely to have a mix of opportunities. Some will involve continuing or expanding in areas that the company is already enjoying, while also opening up new opportunities. This mix is reflected in the different life cycles of opportunities open to the company.

TAKE THE ESSENTIAL NEXT STEP IN YOUR CAREER

Over the years, we have found that a portfolio of competitive advantages is relevant not only at the business unit level, but also at the business function level. We were reminded just how true this is in a meeting with the CEO of a large multinational company, which we will call GlobeCo.

The CEO, Mr. B, was agonizing over the loss of some of his best people, who had left for competitor firms. "What ever happened to loyalty?" he lamented as we met him on the sixtieth floor of a building in the heart of the city. We'd been waiting about 10 minutes, enjoying a spectacular view of one of the world's most beautiful cities, when we were ushered into his office.

It was clear immediately that small talk was not one of Mr. B's strong points. Before we had a chance to sit down, he was telling us about his losses. "We've spent incredible amounts of time and money creating some of the top people in our industry. And I mean that—we created them," he said. "We did it through extensive training and by nurturing their careers from the time they first set foot in this building."

Mr. B and his management team were struggling with something that is becoming a common issue these days—there are not enough high-caliber people at all levels to run increasingly complex businesses in more competitive environments. The issue was getting more attention within GlobeCo, as the leadership team had received its third-quarter report from HR. "The numbers were more alarming than we expected," Mr. B whispered. "We've been losing people faster than we've been able to replace them. It's been gradually depleting our talent pool and affecting our market performance."

We heard that HR's solution was to step up the firm's recruiting efforts and focus more on talent retention. Not happy with this predictable response, Mr. B put together a "root causes" team—a small band of new hires charged with finding out exactly why people were leaving and then coming up with a plan to stem the losses. "I need a few of your people to work with this team," Mr. B informed us. "They are enthusiastic and raring to go, but they need some help in structuring their efforts."

The team moved quickly, reaching out to peers within the company and to strategic resourcing experts. Working with the team, we established that two fundamental trends were having a significant impact on the company:

1. Today's brightest, most talented people tend to pursue careers *across* multiple companies. They want a more varied and challenging career progression than they can hope to find within a single company. This is true even when the company is a strong, iconic global player.

2. Today's top-performing companies generally look for people who have gained experience across multiple companies. Having had a variety of experiences gives people an edge in an increasingly networked business environment.

So, while the best and the brightest were looking for a professional challenge over a three- to five-year time span, GlobeCo was assessing potential hires based on their suitability over the next 40 years. In fact, the company was filtering out the résumés of "job hoppers" because it generally perceived them as being disloyal opportunists.

"It became clear that these people were neither disloyal nor opportunists, but were simply pursuing careers that provided them with essential skills and experiences for this day and age," explained the team leader. "GlobeCo is in desperate need of these people's skills. Imagine the contributions that these people could have made. We might not be in this market situation today if we'd had them aboard earlier, even if only for a few years."

Next on the agenda was to explore how the trends could be turned into an advantage for the company. In a workshop—through ideation, discussion, and ranking—several potential competitive opportunities were identified:

1. Mention challenging "assignments" as well as lifetime career opportunities when advertising positions within the firm. This would make it possible to attract high performers who are seeking suitable career moves rather than lifetime employment.

2. Create distinct salary and benefits packages for those who are pursuing lifetime careers and those who are seeking their next career step. The former would receive slightly lower salaries and more benefits (for example, career development, training, and retirement plans), while the latter would receive higher salaries and limited benefits.

3. Build a corporate capability that would be able to attract, select, bring on board, utilize, and exit substantially larger numbers of people.

Then the discussions took an interesting twist. Several people in the room observed that while GlobeCo was at an obvious disadvantage compared to its peers when trying to hire and retain people for lifetime careers, it had an advantage in that the company offered unique professional assignments. Indeed, the company's substantial change agenda (and backlog) could be turned much more directly into an advantage:

4. Seek top people for professional assignments, hiring individuals directly into the company's change agenda to help reduce the change backlog.

5. Connect with communities of functional "specialists" to help resolve specific transformational challenges and help to make the company more competitive.

The team voted on these five opportunities, prioritizing them in order of importance, with the first one, emphasizing challenging assignments, topping the list. Interestingly, the discussions taking place around the voting revealed that while most people in the room felt intense urgency about stemming the hiring losses, no one thought it was too late. "It was clear at this point that we had control of the situation," Mr. B explained. "We have plenty of professional challenges in our organization, the kind that will attract the best talent. We just hadn't been packaging them right. Instead of offering industry superstars a lifetime career with GlobeCo, we now offer them 'an essential next step in your career.' It's been working beautifully for us."

What Needs to Be Measured?

A well-managed portfolio of competitive opportunities requires a strategic game plan that gives direction to decision making. Evaluating the opportunities requires looking at several dimensions, as shown in Table 3.1.

Portfolio Management and Life-Cycle Tools

In a traditional strategy approach, strategic insights lead directly to decisions on the initiatives needed to address them. The focus tends to be on initiatives because they are easy to measure and manage, and they have a clear return on investment, project charters, appointed teams, milestones, dashboards, and steering committees. Yet, once they are established, initiatives can take on lives of their own, regardless of what is happening in the marketplace. Some initiatives continue to be pursued long after their useful lives have ended. As Rita McGrath points out in her book *The End of Competitive Advantage*, "the fear and sense of career risk often leads managers to cling to eroding businesses long after they should have moved on."[3]

TABLE 3.1

Dimension	Aspect	Typical Questions
Competitiveness	Coherence	How does the competitive opportunity contribute to the overall strategic game plan? How does it create superior customer value? How does it deliver value in an advantaged way? How does it capture value? How does it support other competitive opportunities? How does it strengthen the coherence and completeness of the overall portfolio?
	Life cycle	Where are sources of potential competitive advantage in the life cycle? (Examples might be discovering, growing, exploiting, prolonging, and disengaging—market perspective.)
	Relative importance	How important is this source of potential competitive advantage compared to others (for example, decisive, contributing, or supporting)?
	Company position	Where does the company stand versus traditional and emerging competition in capitalizing on competitive opportunity (for example, leading, on a par with, or lagging)?
Fit	Customer	Does the opportunity contribute to the value proposition for customers? Does it provide them with value beyond what they expect or what they are receiving from competitors?
	Employee	Is the opportunity consistent with organizational capabilities? Does it contribute to employee commitment and passion?
	Financial	Does the opportunity contribute, either directly or indirectly, to the organization's ability to extract growing value from its interaction with customers?
	Operational	Does the opportunity fit the organization's processes and ways of working?
	Technology	Does the opportunity fit with the company's technology base?
Deployment	Effort	What is required in terms of time, effort, and resources to capitalize on the competitive opportunity?
	Interdependency	What is required from other areas of competitive advantage or operations to capitalize on the competitive opportunity?

Organizational Tools Instead of Data Analysis Tools

In managing a portfolio of competitive opportunities, analyses are used not to plot results that are accurate to within two decimal places, but to help create a better and especially a shared understanding of what each of the individual opportunities can contribute to the organization's future. This shared understanding creates a portfolio perspective on how the opportunities relate to the strategic game plan, one another, and their life cycles.

With this in mind, monitoring the entire life cycle of competitive opportunities and their supporting initiatives is a routine aspect of management. They are analyzed, quantified, evaluated, and prioritized in terms of their value, probability, feasibility, and coherence in relation to the overall strategy and to one another. The process of growing and culling opportunities is continual. Eliminating once-useful opportunities is not ad hoc or traumatic because the portfolio provides a systematic framework that ensures that ongoing initiatives are always aiming for the latest competitive goals.

Competitive opportunities are evaluated along two dimensions: their life-cycle stage and their relative strength in the marketplace (see Figure 3.2). There are three life-cycle stages for competitive opportunities:

1. *Emerging and growing* includes the opportunities that form the basis for a company's growing advantage.

2. *Contributing* are opportunities that are the core of the company's current strength.

3. *Declining* are opportunities that are still contributing to the company's success, but are expected to do so less and less.

On the surface, it doesn't seem logical to entertain the notion of a "declining opportunity," but all this means is that an opportunity for creating competitive advantage is eroding in importance. A company,

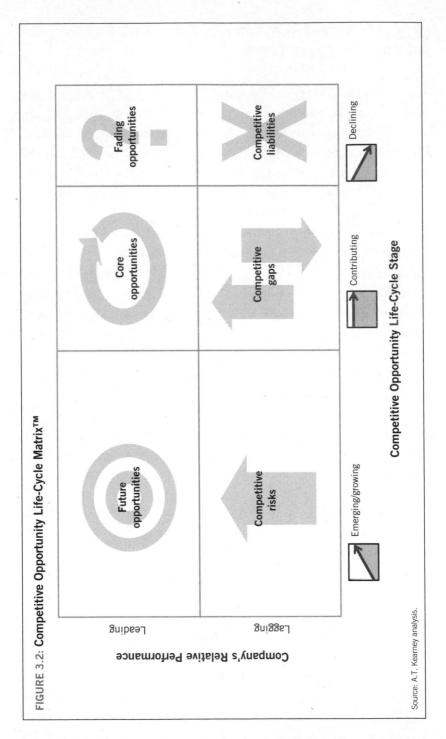

FIGURE 3.2: Competitive Opportunity Life-Cycle Matrix™

Source: A.T. Kearney analysis.

for example, might invest in increasing loyalty among its channel partners to boost its advantage over others, but its channel partners might be under pressure from direct propositions to consumers. A competitive opportunity is indeed like a military mission: it is inspired by the advantage to be gained.

Opportunities are also classified by their leading and lagging performance. Decisions are based on an objective assessment of how the organization is doing relative to its competitors and potential competitors. Such assessments help avoid groupthink, wishful thinking, or C-suite blindness to harsh competitive realities. They also help the company identify competitive risks and gauge the work that lies ahead.

Although such nonquantitative classifications might seem simplistic, keep in mind that their purpose in an involved, cocreative environment is as much about communication and starting a dialogue as it is about analysis. The discussions that take place in determining the classifications raise several questions:

- What are our competitors doing that frustrate our efforts?

- What are we doing that most helps us delight customers and grow the business profitably?

- What competitive opportunities that we are not capitalizing on have substantial potential?

Such questions—when asked of a sufficiently involved cross section of the organization—often provide remarkably rich and revealing insights, and do so in a constructive way. This is difficult, if not impossible, to achieve through detailed data analysis and dissemination.

The Main Courses of Action

The two main dimensions of the life-cycle matrix—the stage in the life cycle and the firm's relative performance—also point to generic courses of action. Much of the attention in strategy is naturally given to the opportunities in the top row of the matrix, where the firm is enjoying true competitive advantage:

Future opportunities. These opportunities will determine the company's future success. As they grow in importance, they must be simultaneously built up and expanded. A typical challenge is dedicating enough time, money, and resources to them relative to today's core strengths. Here, our insurance company might identify the ability to measure and price risk on a real-time basis using technology as a future opportunity.

Core opportunities. These are today's decisive strengths that help provide value to customers and are at the peak of their life cycle. This competitive strength must be fully exploited and ideally kept up to date. Again, our insurance company might list digital processes that put customers in control as a core opportunity.

Fading opportunities. These are opportunities that are approaching the end of their life cycles but are still adding value and thus require a balanced approach—comparing the effort required to prolong each opportunity's life cycle with the benefits achieved. This means evaluating the decline in these opportunities' contribution to the company's success against the risk that the decline will occur in a sudden and disruptive manner. Our insurance company, for example, knows that the loyalty it enjoys from insurance brokers is fading as the broker channel is replaced by technology.

It is equally important to deal with competitive opportunities where the firm is lagging:

Competitive risks. Many organizations see potential competitive opportunities for which they are not well positioned. If these opportunities are important for the company's future competitiveness, for other competitive opportunities, or for the proposition toward customers, then the risk should be mitigated. For example, our insurance company knows that turning microcommunities into new forms of risk pooling is not within its areas of expertise. Alternative payment and social networking companies are at the moment better positioned to capitalize on this opportunity. Therefore, the company might mitigate the risk through an acquisition or a partnership.

Competitive gaps. The counterpart to core opportunities is competitive gaps. A gap is an integral part of the strategic playing field that the company is failing to capitalize on, either because other players execute better or because the company is simply not doing its job. The solution is to either execute better or find alternatives that are smarter, better, or different. For example, an insurance company might lag in the ability to use algorithms to draw on larger data sets to assess risk—something that is important for success.

Competitive liabilities. If a competitive opportunity is running a mediocre course or failing but is still part of the company's strategic playing field, it is a liability. For example, transactional call centers continue to struggle to deliver a remarkable customer experience while being outclassed by online self-help sites. The logical course of action is to try to reframe the liability in a way that warrants its continuation. If that's not possible, it should be discontinued.

A Practical Tool for Organizational Inclusiveness

A life-cycle matrix is not a numbers-focused exercise aimed at positioning each opportunity on a continuum. Rather, it is a tool for motivating and supporting an inclusive dialogue and a shared understanding of how competitive opportunities play out over their life cycles and contribute to the company's success. A typical sequence might be as follows:

- Assess whether the competitive opportunities that the team has identified are growing, at strength and contributing, or declining in importance from a market perspective.

- Once the opportunities are classified, fine-tune their positions on the life-cycle axes.

- Ask whether the company is leading the opportunities and thus enjoying an advantage over competitors or whether it is on a par with them or even lagging them.

- Assess the relative importance of the opportunities by altering the size of the bubbles used for the competitive opportunities.

Making such rough classifications can be helpful in creating a shared understanding of a company's strengths and liabilities, both today and in a few years' time.

Putting Competitive Life-Cycle Management Tools to Use

Assembling a portfolio of competitive opportunities requires some serious thought. Again, we will use our insurance company example to illustrate.

Assessing the Fundamental Trends

The strategy team began by assessing the fundamental trends affecting the business. It was clear that brokers' and customers' loyalty was waning. In the past, a strong presence and "A"-player status had always provided repeat business—helped by the fact that in its current form, insurance was still a relatively low-interest item for consumers. The insurance company had always been responsive to brokers, helping them with special requests and services to ensure their loyalty and retain a substantial part of their business. But loyalty had begun to erode as customers began to shop for better deals and automatic continuation of policies dropped off. The firm was beginning to doubt whether the costs associated with the special treatment provided to brokers were justified by the returns.

Identifying Today's Competitive Opportunities

Brand equity. The company is a strong, established player backed by a well-known global brand with value that appeals to many consumers.

Operational excellence. Several years' worth of fruitful business improvement have moved the firm to an advantaged cost and service position.

Digitized and hands-off processes. Straight-through processing provides brokers and consumers with a more efficient and responsive experience (although brokers that dealt with multiple insurance companies would not accommodate different levels of digital integration).

Evaluating Competitive Opportunities Going Forward

Put customers in control. Comparisons with other industries and geographies found that customers expect to be much more in control of the process than they previously had been— whenever and wherever they want.

Virtualize expertise. Customers expect to receive advice throughout the process—through smart applications and wizards that help them determine their real risk mitigation needs and appropriate solutions.

Use technology to make products configurable. Customers do not mind complex products or services as long as they are easy to use. While the prevailing wisdom says that selling insurance online means that products have to be simple, other industries use technology to do exactly the opposite: make more complexity manageable for consumers—from configuring computers to customizing clothing.

Perform real-time risk management. New technologies make it possible to segment and measure risk—such as pay-as-you-drive and pay-how-you-drive car insurance—more dynamically and in some cases in real time.

Use social media to form micromutualities. Social media allows small groups to form in order to share specific risks, similar to traditional mutualities, but in a smaller, more specific, and more flexible way.

Digitizing processes, putting customers in control, virtualizing expertise, and making products configurable are all opportunities that reinforce one another. The company had all the ingredients to create an ecosystem that would be capable of delighting consumers, while also meeting its risk mitigation needs in a cost-effective way. The strategy team provided a perspective on the portfolio of competitive opportunities, shown in Figure 3.3.

Developing the Strategic Game Plan

The leaders exercise control over the strategy process through the selection of fundamental trends, deciding where the biggest opportunities lie based on the company's strengths, culture, and situation. The insurance company's leadership team believed that technology-related trends offered the biggest potential gain in competitiveness. The strategic game plan went something like this: "Technology will allow us to provide our customers with the tailored risk coverage that they need and want for the best possible price."

In selecting this game plan, the leadership team also accepted the need for a transformation in how the organization was managed. The

FIGURE 3.3: **Competitive Opportunity Life-Cycle Matrix™:** Insurance Company Example

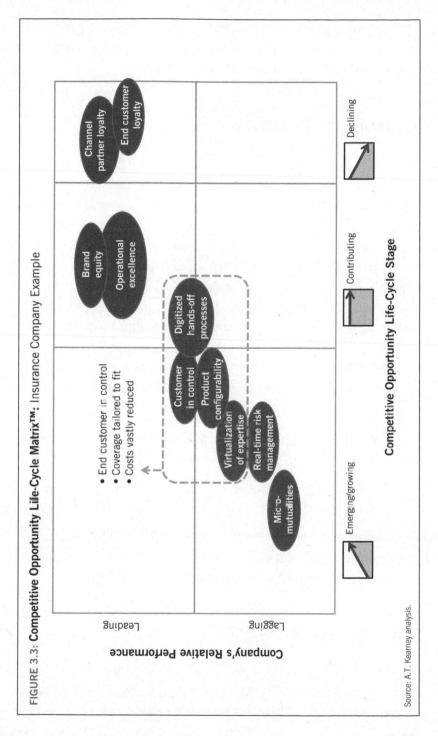

Source: A.T. Kearney analysis.

strategy team's perspective revealed that although the company was in a strong position, a considerable transformation would be needed if it was to remain strong and relevant to customers.

Patterns and Priorities

The conclusions drawn by the insurance company's strategy team about the overall competitive situation are not unusual for companies in previously stable business environments. Newfound strategic freedom—whether it comes from new technology, globalization, or deregulation—can quickly create a step change in ways to delight customers and deliver value. When faced with this prospect, not all companies are in the same situation or react in the same structured fashion as the insurance company. In fact, it is not unusual for companies to find themselves in one of four other situations (see Figure 3.4):

Flounder. Companies go into a frenzy, start chasing competitive opportunities without a clear focus, and quickly become overwhelmed by complexity.

Coast. Companies enter a state of denial and just keep doing what they have been doing, hoping that things will turn out all right.

Disruptors. Innovative upstarts dominate one or a few fast-growing competitive opportunities, disrupting the status quo.

Ride the life cycle. Companies systematically tackle the strategic challenge, figure out which competitive opportunities to focus on, and then embrace the future and ride the life cycles.

Maintaining the Portfolio

A portfolio of competitive opportunities is not static. New technology appears. Customer expectations evolve. The competition refuses to stand still. New fundamental trends take center stage or become

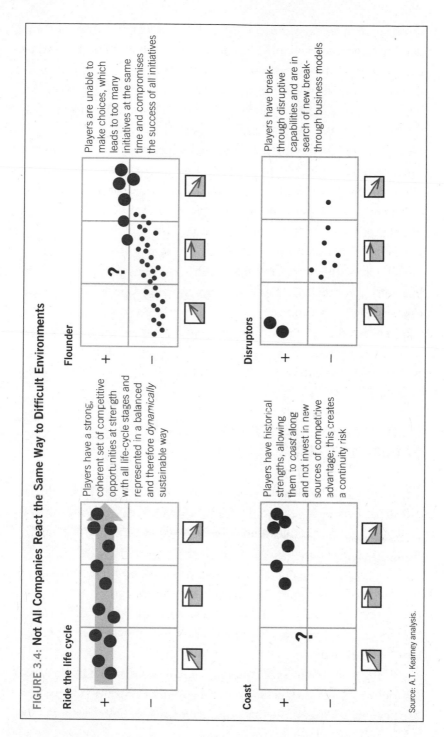

FIGURE 3.4: Not All Companies React the Same Way to Difficult Environments

Ride the life cycle

Players have a strong, coherent set of competitive opportunities at strength with all life-cycle stages and represented in a balanced and therefore *dynamically* sustainable way

Flounder

Players are unable to make choices, which leads to too many initiatives at the same time and compromises the success of all initiatives

Coast

Players have historical strengths, allowing them to *coast* along and not invest in new sources of competitive advantage; this creates a continuity risk

Disruptors

Players have break-through disruptive capabilities and are in search of new break-through business models

Source: A.T. Kearney analysis.

91

more aggressive. Even those who work toward capitalizing on competitive opportunities can fail to act fast enough and lose ground to the competition. What this means is that the portfolio of competitive opportunities must be reviewed regularly and maintained consistently. The portfolio is maintained both from the top down and from the bottom up. On the one hand, the portfolio is defined by the strategic game plan—finding the winning recipe for capitalizing on the fundamental trends that are coming the company's way. On the other hand, important feedback on what works and what doesn't is captured during the initiatives that bring the opportunities to life. This bidirectional input helps keep the portfolio up to date and forward looking. Even ongoing initiatives can turn into strategic initiatives when they are aligned with competitive opportunities. Managing the portfolio becomes a process of continual experimentation, especially in the case of emerging opportunities.

In effect, the strength of strategy comes from putting *all* the pieces together in a coherent way and anticipating what is coming. Let's turn now to an example of competitive life cycles in action.

Pharmaceuticals: Managing the Life Cycle of Competitive Opportunities

The pharmaceutical industry, with companies such as Merck, Pfizer, Novartis, Bristol-Myers Squibb, SmithKline Beecham, and others, provides a good example of how the life cycles of competitive opportunities can play out.

For years, success in this industry was built on the large players' R&D capabilities. Competitive opportunities rested on the discovery of new molecules—to reduce human suffering, preferably in large therapeutic treatment areas—and successfully getting them through clinical trials to the markets.

Things changed in 1984 when the Hatch-Waxman Act made it easier for generic drug makers to enter the market. Within 10 years, the use of generic drugs more than doubled to almost half the market for countable drugs.[4] New technologies also boosted R&D productivity and reduced research sample size requirements. This opened the door to smaller companies entering the drug discovery and development business. Before long, competitor drugs were appearing on the market sooner, not only reducing a new drug's period of exclusivity, but also being introduced before significant returns had been generated.

Shifting Advantage

Competitive opportunity shifted from big R&D to partnering with the smaller drug discovery and development companies in an effort to create more attractive pipelines of drugs in development. Research efficiency and speedier clinical trial processes to get drugs approved also became much more important sources of competitive advantage.

Marketing

The changes didn't stop there, however. Higher healthcare costs and tougher healthcare reforms put pressure on prices. Prescribing doctors typically stayed with name brands for comfort and practical reasons, but cost pressures fueled the substitution of more affordable drugs. This triggered new competitive opportunities, including marketing and advertising directly to consumers. It also made clinical trial phase V testing a potential source of competitive advantage. Phase V testing involves large groups of patients using FDA-approved drugs. The tests provide more consumer-marketable results—for example, revealing which drugs prevent more deaths.

Licensing

With the shift toward sales and marketing, the need to dominate specific therapeutic categories grew in importance. The pharmaceutical companies went beyond collaborating with smaller drug companies to fill their pipelines and also licensed and sold approved drugs in collaboration with them. With more than 50 percent of on-patent drugs now licensed, licensing has turned into an important competitive opportunity.

Lifestyle Drugs

Given the pressure on prices and increasing competition, the playing field expanded to lifestyle drugs, epitomized by the erectile dysfunction treatment drug Viagra. It reached sales of more than $1 billion within the first year of its launch, making it the most successful drug introduction ever. Clearly, lifestyle drugs were an important new competitive opportunity.

This is just a small sample of the industry's developments over the past 40 years. But it does highlight the life cycles of competitive opportunities as they move from emerging to contributing, and ultimately to fading.

CHAPTER 4

How the Principles Work Together

Having a strategy suggests an ability to look up from the short term and the trivial to view the long term and the essential, to address causes rather than symptoms, to see woods rather than trees.

—LAWRENCE FREEDMAN[1]

OUR FUTUREPROOF METHODOLOGY for reclaiming strategy synthesizes three powerful principles, which, in combination, set it apart from twentieth-century approaches to strategy:

1. Draw inspiration from the future.

2. Be organizationally inclusive.

3. Take a portfolio approach.

The methodology plays out at three levels: develop a game plan, identify competitive opportunities, and execute initiatives to capture these opportunities. All three levels are managed within the framework and boundaries set by top management.

Essentially, we are talking about two related journeys: One is about developing a strategy with the help of the organization; the other is a metadrive toward embracing new ways to manage strategy. Together, the two journeys lead to a new competitive strategy that, with the help of organizational learning by doing, comes together to manage strategy on an ongoing basis. Strategy becomes the organization's "new normal." The game plan, the competitive opportunities, and the initiatives are maintained so that the formulation and deployment of strategy go hand in hand.

Let's consider the five-stage process for developing and implementing a strategy (see Figure 4.1):

Aim. The leadership arms itself to guide the organization through the process of creating or reviewing its strategy by developing the game plan to direct the strategic efforts.

Inspire. The organization's collective and distributed knowledge, insights, tacit understanding, and expertise are used to translate fundamental trends into competitive opportunities.

Evaluate. Competitive opportunities are detailed, scrutinized to ensure that they are viable, realistic, attractive, achievable, mutually reinforcing, and consistent with the strategic game plan, and then decided on.

Initiate. Competitive opportunities are matched to concrete initiatives; other ongoing initiatives that distract from or do not contribute to the opportunities and the strategic game plan are adapted or culled.

Embed. The organization's ways of working change in order to manage the strategic game plan, the portfolio of competitive opportunities, and the strategic initiatives.

As Figure 4.1 illustrates, FutureProof strategy is very different from traditional linear strategy:

1. Extensive preparation in the Aim stage gives leaders the means (and the shared conviction) to guide organizational inclusive-

FIGURE 4.1: **Typical Stages in FutureProof Strategies**

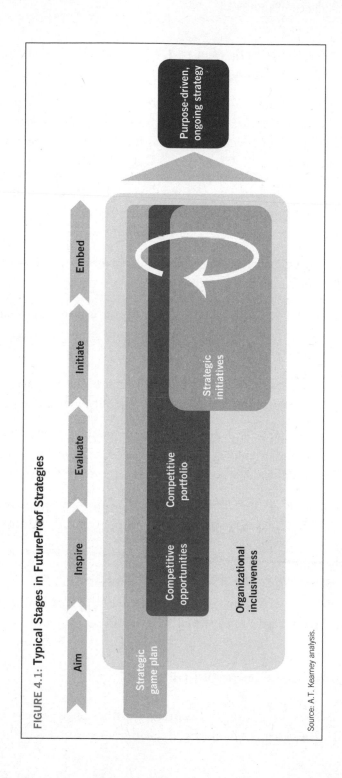

Source: A.T. Kearney analysis.

ness; this is captured in a strategic game plan that is used and maintained throughout the effort.

2. Organizational inclusiveness begins at a very early point so that fundamental trends, in combination with tacit knowledge and firsthand experience rather than analysis of the past, can become sources of strategic insight.

3. Strategy is managed on three levels: the strategic game plan, a portfolio of competitive opportunities, and a set of strategic initiatives to capitalize on those opportunities.

   • The game plan drives the long-term direction and reinforces the company's purpose.

   • The portfolio of competitive opportunities combines the longer term with the here and now and is managed over time.

   • The strategic initiatives provide the agility necessary to keep the strategy valid in a rapidly changing environment.

4. Insights are derived from the fundamental trends, then analyzed and evaluated. This allows for broader and more future-oriented strategic insights as well as more focused analyses.

5. Strategy is a means to continually manage the company more strategically and to provide a guiding organizational energy.

The outcome of a FutureProof strategy is not only a new competitive strategy but also a much more future-aware and anticipatory organization that owns the outcome. This creates both the opportunity and the need to manage strategy in a different, more continuous way.

FutureProof Strategy in Action

We will use a case study to illustrate how these five stages work in real life. The case of C-Bank has all the ingredients necessary to show

how a FutureProof strategy emerges, step-by-step, in a hectic business environment. It includes both the excitement of discovery and the pain of unlearning old practices and assumptions.[2]

The History of C-Bank

This is the story of the commercial division of a large, established banking group that we have called C-Bank. The bank serves small and medium-size enterprises (SMEs) in the developed world. It has served its medium-size clients for decades by providing business, commercial, and property loans as well as a variety of account and international payment services and basic treasury services.

Like most banks, C-Bank was dealt a serious blow by the global financial crisis. Regulatory changes forced banks to be more prudent in their use of capital and to deleverage their balance sheets. Since the start of the crisis, business loans—the mainstay of C-Bank's business—had dropped by more than 20 percent. Loan defaults had also gone up. In addition, more stringent lending criteria had slowed C-Bank's business, which was unfortunate because intrinsic demand for SME loans had increased. These businesses now faced tougher market conditions and had less capability to self-finance their growth. C-Bank's loan rejection rates had skyrocketed—from less than 5 percent outright rejections to more than 25 percent. The bank also suspected that many businesses weren't even bothering to ask for loans anymore.

Management saw no signs of market improvement in the foreseeable future. C-Bank would continue to face cost pressure, as it was spending significant amounts of resources looking for SMEs that met its lending criteria and developing other products and services to serve them. Making matters worse, the public held banks in general in low regard because of the industry's perceived role in triggering the financial crisis.

C-Bank also faced an array of technology-based competitors that were targeting what had previously been exclusive commercial bank offerings. Peer-to-peer lending and crowdfunding startups were intruding on lending. New mobile players, backed by large telecom operators, were making inroads into payment services, and e-commerce was increasingly being facilitated by new transaction service providers such as Amazon. Although often still very small, these upstarts were making banks look outdated and out of step with clients' rising expectations.

The Need for a Strategy

C-Bank's CEO was concerned that his people were working harder, but getting fewer results as business and client appreciation continued to fall. He understood that the bank needed a new strategy to give it a renewed relevance and a more attractive future. The strategy would have to go beyond smarter use of capital or clever accommodation of regulatory changes. Corporate headquarters was already doing everything possible to enhance the bank's competitiveness in these areas. An effective strategy would need to focus on serving current and future clients with products and services that fit their needs. If the strategy could do this, it would also lift the spirits of the staff.

The Strategy Team: Clearing the Decks

After discussions with the leadership team, the CEO formed a strategy team, made up of 15 employees from various levels across the organization. Consultants from a strategy consulting firm were brought in, not to develop C-Bank's new strategy but to support, moderate, and challenge the new strategy team. The intent was to pursue a strategy by making use of the organization's knowledge and experience.

The first stumbling block emerged before the project even began. Like many organizations that are attempting to address strategy, the bank lacked the capacity to think systematically and rigorously about the future. Employees were already overloaded by the day-to-day business, along with an array of ongoing initiatives.

So instead of launching into creating a new strategy, the first order of business was to take stock of the ongoing initiatives. "We would have to do this at some point during the effort anyway," explained a team leader. "And stopping or adapting some of the initiatives would free up resources to think systematically about the future."

The team began by reviewing the pipeline of ongoing and planned initiatives to determine what was being done and why. As information was collected, it became clear that there was little shared purpose or consistency among the initiatives. The vast majority of them had to do with incremental or even housekeeping activities, such as changes in the bank's products, services, systems, and ways of working, either as a result of regulatory changes or simply to keep up with market developments.

It didn't take long for the team to realize that some projects were counterproductive. For example, an initiative to reduce IT-related project costs was not even remotely compatible with an initiative to develop more flexible products. Other initiatives had vague goals, such as the perennial instructions from headquarters to "become more customer-centric."

Clearing the decks was initially expected to take three weeks, but it ended up taking almost two months. However, the time wasn't wasted. Initiatives that were not crucial were stopped, including a new branch format, an employee scheduling system, and a new pricing strategy, as well as some "lip service" projects that consisted mainly of regular cross-department meetings with little to show for them. Some initiatives were focused on improving processes that should be replaced, such as a "call center–customer touchpoint improvement project" when the real solution should be to create an online environment where customers could take care of their own needs.

With fewer initiatives, C-Bank now had the capacity to formulate a FutureProof strategy.

Getting Started: Aim

The first stage is for the leaders to understand the nature of the bank's competitive situation, get a feel for the general direction of where the organization should be heading, and prepare a first draft of the strategic game plan.

The leaders take ownership of the process by setting the parameters for the strategic journey. The challenge is to articulate a compelling direction that is both inspirational and guiding. This doesn't mean that the leaders have all the answers. On the contrary, finding the answers is what organizational inclusiveness is all about.

The most pragmatic way of doing so is to think in terms of fundamental trends. As discussed in Chapter 2, these trends are predictable, long-term shifts that are affecting the company now or could affect it in the future. In guiding the organization in strategy formulation, leaders choose the trends that they believe are most important and then outline how the company can take advantage of them or fend off their negative impact where necessary.

Selecting the fundamental trends and defining how the company can take advantage of them is how leaders maintain control of organizationally inclusive strategy formulation. It ensures that the trends are relevant to the company and consistent with one another. The leaders thus provide a clear context, boundaries, direction, and inspiration.

The Aim stage typically has several outcomes:

- A strategy team, including leaders, that is prepared, committed, and able to lead the organization on its strategic journey

- A definition of what "winning" means to establish the overall strategic goals and ambitions (This can be numbers-based or expressed in terms of other measurable achievements.)

- A general strategic game plan:

  - A list of the fundamental trends that will be most important for the company

  - An outline of how the company will take advantage of these trends

- The design of the inclusive journey—for example, in what order will the challenges and questions be addressed? What intermediate results will be aimed for?

- A plan for managing organizational inclusion—for example, which parts of the organization should be included and when? Who should be invited, and how should their inclusion be managed? Which collaborative environment will be used?

- A kick-off event to launch the organization's inclusion

At this stage, the details are still general. The leaders have not yet defined value propositions or new business models. For example, C-Bank wanted to look into using technology to create a richer product offering while simultaneously putting customers in control of their own affairs at much lower cost levels—in its words, to provide "corporate banking richness with retail banking convenience."

Importantly, the outcome of the Aim stage must be a leadership team that is committed to a strategic game plan so that it can guide and inspire organizational inclusiveness. Without this, inclusion is likely to backfire, leaving a more cynical and disillusioned workforce.

The Business Opportunity

C-Bank considered SMEs a real business opportunity. They make up a major part of the economy, but because of their large numbers and small size, they can be difficult to serve. The leadership decided to draw on two major sources of insights and launched two teams: the fundamental trends team and the competitive baseline team.

The *fundamental trends team* was made up of 15 young, high-potential employees who worked with the consultants to identify the most important trends that will affect the business. The team was to provide insights into two types of trends: those that will affect SME clients directly and those that will affect the overall banking business (especially those that are technology-related).

The team members began researching reports, white papers, trend analyses, and other material about SME banking, financial services, and other related industries and identified the trends that would be affecting the bank going forward. Then, in two workshops with the extended leadership team, these trends were ultimately winnowed down to those that were deemed most important for the bank.

The *competitive baseline team* was made up of 10 people from different levels in marketing, sales, and strategy who, together with the consultants, were charged with gathering information about both traditional competitors and the new players and startups that were making inroads into financial services.

The team came up with some interesting insights. Traditional competitors were not doing things differently or better—but they weren't doing particularly badly either. The new players and startups were pursuing a variety of new financial services and related offerings. Most of these were consumer focused but could easily be extended to SMEs. As a disclaimer, the team explained that most of the examples were still small and might not be successful, but they nevertheless showed that offerings might soon look very different. (The team did not spend time on projecting detailed segment-specific market shares into the future or other deterministic attempts to handle future uncertainties.)

It soon became clear that lessons in organizational decision making were needed. For example, the team had to learn that inclusion is not the same as "deciding by committee." Consensus is not always possible, likely, or desirable. However, participants were excited about being an integral part of the process. Over the course of the project, a modus operandi was found. The starting point was always a sounding of the strategy team followed, later on, by broader organizational inclusion using voting and other simple ways to express the group's collective judgment. Important decisions remained the leadership's responsibility, but the reasons for those decisions were widely shared. As a result, participants could see that the decisions made sense, and most of them remained fully engaged.

Involving a broad range of people has its costs. Some people had a hard time leaving their comfort zones and overcoming the tendency to rest on their accomplishments. The challenge was to get people to imagine new sources of competitive opportunities, despite the bank's long history, ingrained beliefs, and established ways of working. It was not enough for consultants to tell them about these opportunities. For the insights to become real and energizing, the participants had to discover them for themselves. The collaborative process helped this along, as peers began to challenge one another.

Paradoxically, some participants wanted to jump in and do everything all at once. Some took ownership of their part of the strategic puzzle and were eager to get started, without taking the time to understand the bigger picture. They were confident that their domain contained "the answer." It took time for them to see the benefits of a game plan that integrated all the elements to provide clear direction about what to do and when to do it and how all the pieces fit together.

Before C-Bank moved on to the Inspire stage, each of the questions on the following checklist had a "yes" answer:

- Have the most important fundamental trends been selected?

- Have we defined how the company can take advantage of them?

- Have we defined where not to go?

- Is there a clear plan for the inclusive journey?

- Is our strategic game plan forward-looking enough to be truly inspirational?

Exploring the Future: Inspire

In this stage, the collective firsthand experience with customers, markets, partners, and processes, along with the tacit knowledge of staff members throughout the organization, is called upon in a guided, inclusive journey. The goal is to formulate and prioritize opportunities for competitive advantage.

The Inspire stage typically has several outcomes:

- Shared insights concerning the important and relevant fundamental trends in the industry that help the company anticipate the future

- A coherent set of discrete competitive opportunities, identified as attainable sources of competitive advantage that will put and keep the company in a leading position (These opportunities are scrutinized and prepared for decision making during the Evaluate stage.)

- A well-articulated strategic game plan to inspire the organization and explain why and how the company will succeed

Those preparing the strategy effort at C-Bank consisted of the leadership and members of the strategy, fundamental trends, and competitive baseline teams. This group also planned the Inspire stage, in which an even broader part of the organization would be invited to help assess the implications of the fundamental trends and formulate competitive opportunities.

Preparations focused on three aspects of the strategic journey: creating inspirational material to fuel organizational engagement, planning the steps in the process, and designing the process for inclusion.

Creating the Strategic Journey

The strategic journey is a sequence of interactions that guides the organization as it thinks about and builds on the fundamental trends, determines how to take advantage of them, and then synthesizes them into discrete competitive opportunities. The bank's preferred approach was to begin the conversation using question and interaction (Q&I) cycles, followed by voting and ranking as described in Chapter 3.

Webinars with external experts were organized, and engaging web-based mini-presentations were created to highlight each trend, including using examples from other industries to illustrate what is possible. These examples, in combination with appropriate what-if questions, moved the organization out of its comfort zone. For example, in one conversation, a facilitator asked: "When performing a risk assessment of a loan application, is there a difference between trusting 168 reviewers of a hotel on Booking.com and trusting a large number of positive online reviews from clients of a company selling through Amazon?" When discussing this comparison, the group quickly concluded that online customer reviews provided important information on the performance of a potential client that was relevant to its risk assessment. This was one of many questions used to help participants understand the importance of fundamental trends and how the organization can take advantage of them.

This is also where abductive logic comes into play. Facilitators asked the group to imagine what loan risk assessment would look like if there were more sources of information, such as customer evaluations of the companies that were applying for loans. When asked how likely this was to become true, the group discovered that several such sources were already available and being used. For example, many SMEs use cloud-based bookkeeping solutions that are easily tapped into and evaluated with the help of algorithms and pattern recognition. The competitive baseline team also found several startups that were exploring the use of such information sources to assess risk. In other words, the future was already here—and it was very feasible.

The strategy team also put together a preliminary itinerary for the strategy journey to guide the process. As part of the kickoff, participants posted examples of companies, startups, products, services, or initiatives that they saw as important early signals for commercial banking.

An outline of the journey is depicted in Figure 4.2.

For the Inspire stage, the leaders wanted to expand participation to generate more ideas and help assess the impact of various trends on the company, as well as make a broader cross section of the organization aware of likely future developments.

However, achieving broad participation would not be easy, given the bank's geographic spread. The decision was to assemble a multi-

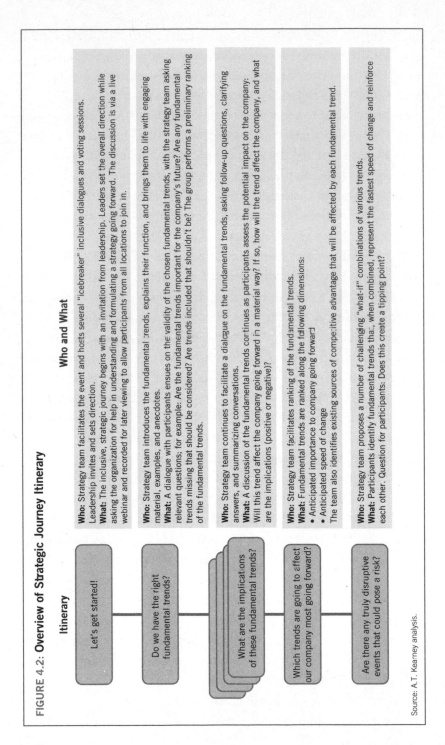

FIGURE 4.2: Overview of Strategic Journey Itinerary

Itinerary

Let's get started!

Do we have the right fundamental trends?

What are the implications of these fundamental trends?

Which trends are going to affect our company most going forward?

Are there any truly disruptive events that could pose a risk?

Who and What

Who: Strategy team facilitates the event and hosts several "icebreaker" inclusive dialogues and voting sessions. Leadership invites and sets direction.
What: The inclusive, strategic journey begins with an invitation from leadership. Leaders set the overall direction while asking the organization for help in understanding and formulating a strategy going forward. The discussion is via a live webinar and recorded for later viewing to allow participants from all locations to join in.

Who: Strategy team introduces the fundamental trends, explains their function, and brings them to life with engaging material, examples, and anecdotes.
What: A dialogue with participants ensues on the validity of the chosen fundamental trends, with the strategy team asking relevant questions; for example: Are the fundamental trends important for the company's future? Are any fundamental trends missing that should be considered? Are trends included that shouldn't be? The group performs a preliminary ranking of the fundamental trends.

Who: Strategy team continues to facilitate a dialogue on the fundamental trends, asking follow-up questions, clarifying answers, and summarizing conversations.
What: A discussion of the fundamental trends continues as participants assess the potential impact on the company: Will this trend affect the company going forward in a material way? If so, how will the trend affect the company, and what are the implications (positive or negative)?

Who: Strategy team facilitates ranking of the fundamental trends.
What: Fundamental trends are ranked along the following dimensions:
• Anticipated importance to company going forward
• Anticipated speed of change
The team also identifies existing sources of competitive advantage that will be affected by each fundamental trend.

Who: Strategy team proposes a number of challenging "what-if" combinations of various trends.
What: Participants identify fundamental trends that, when combined, represent the fastest speed of change and reinforce each other. Question for participants: Does this create a tipping point?

Source: A.T. Kearney analysis.

FIGURE 4.2: **Overview of Strategic Journey Itinerary** (*continued*)

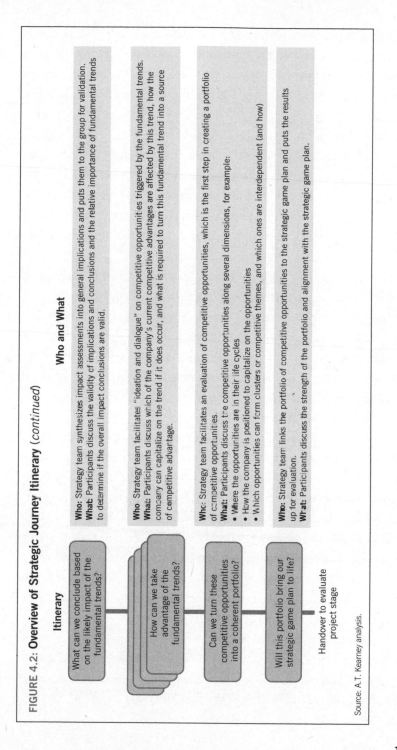

Itinerary

- What can we conclude based on the likely impact of the fundamental trends?

- How can we take advantage of the fundamental trends?

- Can we turn these competitive opportunities into a coherent portfolio?

- Will this portfolio bring our strategic game plan to life?

Handover to evaluate project stage

Who and What

Who: Strategy team synthesizes impact assessments into general implications and puts them to the group for validation.
What: Participants discuss the validity of implications and conclusions and the relative importance of fundamental trends to determine if the overall impact conclusions are valid.

Who: Strategy team facilitates "ideation and dialogue" on competitive opportunities triggered by the fundamental trends.
What: Participants discuss which of the company's current competitive advantages are affected by this trend, how the company can capitalize on the trend if it does occur, and what is required to turn this fundamental trend into a source of competitive advantage.

Who: Strategy team facilitates an evaluation of competitive opportunities, which is the first step in creating a portfolio of competitive opportunities.
What: Participants discuss the competitive opportunities along several dimensions, for example:
- Where the opportunities are in their life cycles
- How the company is positioned to capitalize on the opportunities
- Which opportunities can form clusters or competitive themes, and which ones are interdependent (and how)

Who: Strategy team links the portfolio of competitive opportunities to the strategic game plan and puts the results up for evaluation.
What: Participants discuss the strength of the portfolio and alignment with the strategic game plan.

Source: A.T. Kearney analysis.

disciplinary group across hierarchies, largely self-selected, to ensure enthusiasm for the project. Yet for some people on the strategy team, broadening participation beyond "the usual suspects," or people who were close to and trusted by the leadership team, required a change in mindset.

The inclusion process began with all three teams—strategy, fundamental trends, and competitive baseline—selecting people to participate. To broaden inclusiveness, each participant was asked to invite five more people. The only requirement was that invitees had to be willing and able to make useful contributions. Participants were encouraged to invite both seasoned and inexperienced people, and both recent hires and long-time employees.

The result was a group of about 150 people from different geographic locations, functions, departments, tenures, and hierarchies. The total number of participants was much larger than typical to ensure that the group had sufficient capacity to tackle the challenge. For example, participants included people with experience at other banks and in other industries; this was essential for creating the open-mindedness necessary to explore opportunities without getting stuck in ingrained assumptions and dogmas.

Because of the geographic spread and time constraints, discussions were conducted in online collaborative environments. Virtual meeting platforms provided a central location for materials, a way to capture the richness of the interaction among participants, and a means of voting on and ranking options along the way.

This viral—but selective—inclusiveness was well suited for the explorative strategic process that the leadership team had in mind. (Broader mobilization would have been appropriate if the outcome had been known up front or if performance improvement had had to be addressed more explicitly.)

Roles were also assigned to various subgroups. The initial strategy and competitive baseline teams were in charge of facilitating the strategy journey and the inclusion process. The fundamental trends team was asked to continue "owning" the fundamental trends and to help bring them to life.

The Fundamental Trends

In the process of exploring the fundamental trends, the group felt that some trends were missing from those that had been initially selected by the leadership and the strategy team. After several discussions, an additional trend was put forward for consideration: "always on." This was considered important for two reasons:

- Clients expected the bank to be "always on" for business. Tolerance for waiting times was evaporating, as customers expected instant responses to requests and the ability to take care of their own affairs.

- Products and services had to be "real time." Rather than being set up at the beginning and remaining the same over the duration of the contract, products would follow clients' needs or situations dynamically over time. For example, if solvency was a criterion for granting a loan, why shouldn't it be tracked and used to adjust loan interest rates on an ongoing basis?

As a result, "always on" became the ninth fundamental trend on the list.

Trend 5, digitization, also led to intense discussions. Several people felt that digitization was not one trend but several that should be separated. In the end, it was kept as a single trend, but with off-shoots that indicated the ways in which digitization played out along the way. For example, digitization can make a process more efficient (by eliminating the need for human involvement) and also make complexity manageable by allowing for cost-effective product configuration and tailoring.

Through several rounds of voting, the fundamental trends were ranked on their likely relative importance to the bank and their speed of change as a proxy for the likely opportunities for creating advantage. The matrix in Figure 4.3 shows the high-impact trends selected by the leadership. It also shows some of the fundamental trends that the leadership had deemed to be less relevant and had already filtered

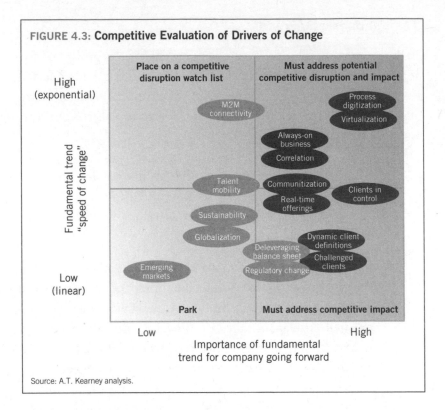

FIGURE 4.3: Competitive Evaluation of Drivers of Change

Source: A.T. Kearney analysis.

out during the Aim stage. The leadership team decided that trends related to demographics, regulatory change, and balance sheets were secondary.

Identifying Competitive Opportunities

The next thing on the agenda was to translate the fundamental trends into discrete competitive opportunities, including how the trends could affect the bank's current sources of competitive advantage. Each opportunity would have to be described, turned into concrete goals, and pursued in a coordinated fashion.

The process involved asking two questions: What would the firm's competitive advantage look like if this trend were fully exploited? What would be required in terms of other capabilities or fundamental trends?

Questions of abductive logic were also explored: What is the likelihood of this trend materializing? What would have to happen for it to materialize? (The answers to these questions helped to identify relationships between fundamental trends.) And how likely is it that these happenings would actually materialize?

The competitive opportunities were then put into clusters that reinforced each other, as shown in Table 4.1.

In answering these questions, the leaders observed that the bank's current ways of working, or even an improved version, were not mentioned. This confirmed their fear that they were not just going through a tough period that would resolve over time, but were instead facing a continuing transformation challenge that would require reconsidering fundamental assumptions about how the bank was operating. It also clarified the implications of these trends for the current business. Over the past few years, efforts to make the bank's traditional offerings and processes more competitive had yielded results, but it became clear that the bank would not enjoy the fruits of these efforts for very long. Competitiveness was now determined by the bank's ability to provide a fully digitized commercial banking environment in which customers could take care of their own affairs.

Also, the abductive logic questions led to new and creative ideas. One idea concerned community guarantees—a sort of escrow savings account in which investors get an attractive interest rate and the bank gets some protection against default on the business loan. For example, the SME finds parties to vouch for its business and its loan application. These parties are offered a higher interest rate on an escrow savings account with a guaranteed percentage payout when the loan is repaid. If the business fails, the parties get some of the interest that was paid on the loan, but they lose their savings. Such guarantees reduce the bank's risk (by outsourcing risk assessment to parties that are in a better position to judge the loan applicant's riskiness) and help reduce the bank's loan default rate.

TABLE 4.1

Fundamental Trends	Competitive Opportunities	Most Important Requirements
1. *Challenged clients* facing adverse conditions	Offer low-cost, convenient traditional products and services Provide efficient, cost-effective traditional banking operations	
2. *Clients in control* and managing their own affairs	Provide self-administered banking offerings and environment	End-to-end digitized and "human-free" processes Ability to provide necessary advice and support
3. *Dynamically defined clients* that work in partnerships and ecosystems	Develop alternative forms of risk assessment and mitigation to serve smaller and one-project clients Create corporate banking–style products and services for SMEs Take on multiclient and one-project products and services Provide a multiclient and one-project self-administered environment	
4. *Always-on banking* open for business	Maintain 24/7 self-administered banking offerings Maintain 24/7 self-administered advice, guidance, and environment	End-to-end digitized and "human-free" processes

5. *Digitization* of processes and information	Develop end-to-end digitized and "human-free" processes with low-cost scalability	Self-administered processes for clients Ability to provide consistent advice and support Algorithm-driven risk assessment and decision-making process Algorithm-driven process to monitor new data usage
6. *Virtualization* of knowledge, expertise, and advice	Provide self-administered, tailored advice and guidance to clients	Algorithm-driven process to monitor new data usage
7. *"Communalization"* and growing social fabric	Perform social capital–driven risk assessment and mitigation Use community guarantees to mitigate risk	
8. *Algorithmic intelligence* drawing on increasing data availability	Exploit alternative data sources to fuel algorithm-driven "human-free" risk assessment and decision making	
9. *Real-time offerings* adapting to changing conditions and needs	Provide incentives to minimize risk exposure Ensure the ability to price offerings dynamically	

Ranking the Opportunities

Two rankings were performed. Competitive opportunities were plotted based on their life cycle stages as declining, contributing, or emerging and growing. Then the situation for each opportunity was compared to traditional and potential competitors. The discussions led to a designation of the following competitive life cycles (see Figure 4.4):

> *Declining.* Traditional bank processes managed by people and involving transactions focused on stable, growing, and low-risk clients
>
> *Horizon 1: contributing.* Self-administered, "human-free" commercial banking fueled by algorithm-based risk assessment and decision making that draws on alternative data sources and social capital (This would provide fully developed *direct commercial bank* capabilities so that clients can handle their own banking affairs conveniently, efficiently, and cost-effectively with minimal involvement of C-Bank's people.)
>
> *Horizon 2: growing.* A corporate banking–style offering for a more complex business environment, drawing on alternative forms of active risk management and mitigation (This would provide *corporate banking richness* in terms of the variety of products available; it would be similar to corporate banking.)
>
> *Horizon 3: emerging.* A rich multicompany offering for a dynamic business environment (This would provide *facilitating ecosystems and communities*, turning the bank into an SME ecosystem capable of facilitating networked and community-driven activities.)

In discussing the timing associated with the three horizons, it was determined that Horizon 1 had already started, Horizon 2 would have to become reality within a couple of years, and Horizon 3 would take more than three years. More important, however, it became clear that

FIGURE 4.4: **Competitive Opportunity Life-Cycle Matrix™:** Commercial Bank Example

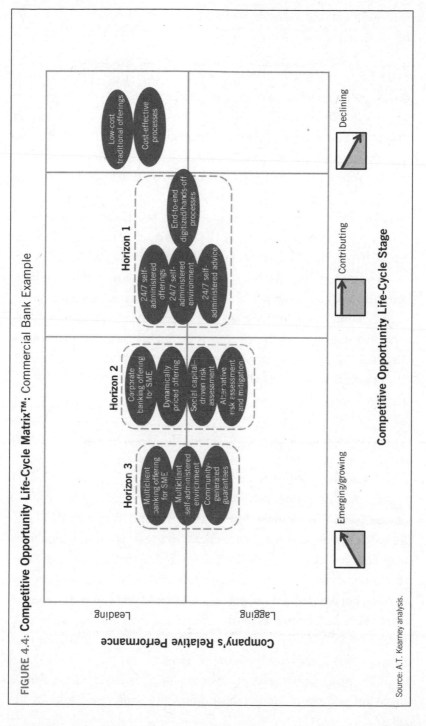

Source: A.T. Kearney analysis.

this could not be a sequential effort. The entire portfolio would have to be top of mind when it came to directing strategic initiatives. Changes to IT systems and customer-facing processes, for example, would have to be made with both Horizon 2 and Horizon 3 in mind to capitalize on the potential within a reasonable time frame.

It was difficult to agree on where the opportunities stood in relation to competitors. The online dialogues failed to come together, the scoring ranges were very wide, and it was hard to assess competitive opportunities that had not yet been exploited by anyone in the market. In the end, the group agreed to postpone the ranking, except for the areas of community-generated guarantees, social capital–driven risk assessment, alternative forms of risk assessment and mitigation, and 24/7 self-administered advice and guidance.

It was clear that startups were making headway by using communities and social capital for alternative risk management purposes. And C Bank was definitely lagging in providing self-administered advice and guidance, and in algorithm-based risk assessments that draw on new and alternative data sources.

For traditional SME banking offerings and processes, C-bank was ahead of other players, but this capability was becoming less important. The decision was made to revisit the ranking efforts during the Evaluation stage, after individual competitive opportunities had been detailed and more information would be available.

Discussions about relative competitiveness also revealed that C-Bank had been underestimating the potential of several nonbank competitors. For example, PayPal and Amazon were already closely linked to SMEs and their customers, processing large numbers of transactions between them and accumulating vast amounts of information on customers. Both companies offered, or had the potential to offer, corporate banking products (such as conditional payments, lines of credit, guarantees, and escrow accounts) and had systems in place to administer syndicated loans, project finance, and other multicompany financial products and services.

The group conversations also explored what offerings for the three horizons would look like and how the bank could take advantage of the fundamental trends. The output of these conversations was captured in scenarios that showed what the future could look like in terms of products and services. Several subgroups formed and became expert motivators, encouraging members to come up with the most attractive offerings.

Guiding the Inclusion

Throughout the Inspire stage, participants explored the potential opportunities and how they might contribute to C-Bank's overall strategic game plan. Members of the strategy team facilitated these discussions to make sure that everyone stayed focused on creating relevant opportunities. The facilitators struck a balance between guiding the discussion and leaving it open enough to reveal unexpected issues and opportunities. Voting and rankings were helpful in "normalizing" the loudest voices by situating strong opinions within the perspective of the group as a whole.

Crunching the Numbers: Evaluate

Traditional strategy approaches draw their inspiration from analyzing and extrapolating data and information. By contrast, FutureProof strategy analyzes and substantiates future possibilities.

In the Evaluate stage, all designated competitive opportunities are analyzed and assessed in terms of what it would take to make them happen. Traditional strategy tools, analyses, and business plan approaches can be used, but with one difference: organizational inclusiveness is used to ensure realism, achievability, and relevance of a formal go or no-go decision.

The Evaluate stage typically has the following outcomes:

- A set of substantiated and evaluated competitive opportunities

- A validated portfolio life-cycle perspective on these opportunities

- Go or no-go decisions about the pursuit of individual opportunities

- Portfolio management principles, captured in the strategic game plan

Decision Making

When making decisions at this stage, all competitive opportunities are first substantiated through individual business cases that outline the risks and benefits of the opportunity and what is required to address it in terms of time, effort, and money. The process also addresses the interdependencies of each opportunity with other competitive opportunities and the synergies to be enjoyed upon implementation.

All decisions must be consistent with the strategic game plan, as it provides the rationale for linking competitive opportunities and making judgments about their relative importance. Organizational inclusiveness is vital at this stage so that the strategic game plan and the substantiation of competitive opportunities benefit from multidisciplinary attention and are *owned* by the organization. The strategic game plan can't belong only to the leadership. It has to become the guiding force for everyone in the organization.

Too Much to Handle?

The Inspire stage had provided C-Bank executives with information about what lay ahead and the challenges involved. The teams could see not only the bank's future, but also the amount of work that would have to be done to make even the first part of the three-horizon strategy a reality. It was clear that performing the associated detail work in one step was a stretch.

The leaders therefore decided to expand organizational inclusiveness gradually and break down the evaluation stage into several parts. They created the necessary decision-making support to identify the most important components of the strategy, followed by successive efforts to add detail to the competitive opportunities, beginning with Horizon 1. These follow-on projects gradually drew in more people as required.

The following areas were explored:

- **Intrinsic market potential.** The larger the intrinsic SME demand for traditional banking products such as loans, the more attractive the bank's strategy would become. C-Bank expected latent demand to be considerable, especially from smaller clients.

- **Alternative SME banking products and services.** Investment in self-administered, corporate banking–style products and multiclient offerings would have to be justified by demand. This required investigating what these products could look like and testing them in the marketplace, while understanding that market research on products and services that do not yet exist is difficult.

- **Alternative risk assessment and mitigation approaches.** Some opportunities depended on the ability to innovate in the area of risk assessment, first by drawing on new sources of data and information and then by mitigating risk with new approaches to guarantees. The leaders had to know, and soon, whether such risk management innovations were realistic, since so much was depending on them.

The strategy team compiled a list of competitive opportunities to be investigated before committing resources to the effort, then sent that list over to the team members to evaluate, with support from the consultants and the fundamental trends team. Several members of the strategy team facilitated the effort to make sure that the outcome remained properly focused. As they explored the issues, the team members steadily gained more insight concerning what was happening in the marketplace. As a result, they were able to refine the life-cycle matrix of competitive opportunities.

The teams also began to detail and evaluate competitive opportunities within Horizon 1 along the following dimensions:

- *What is it?* What does the competitive opportunity entail? What will it do? What difference will it make for clients? How does it compare to what is being done today?

- *Benefits.* What benefits does the competitive opportunity provide? Can these benefits be quantified? If so, how do they stack up? Will clients experience these benefits as a jump forward?

- *Differentiation.* Will this provide differentiation in the market, or is it necessary simply to stay in the game? Is there a window of opportunity to consider, and if so, how long will this window last? Will it create more client convenience, a better product and service fit with client needs, more cost-effective delivery, or lower prices?

- *Transformation.* What will this competitive opportunity require in terms of transforming the value chain? Can the effort required for this transformation be estimated in terms of timing, general effort, people, systems, costs, and investments? Can the transformation be obtained externally instead of being built in-house?

- *Interdependencies.* Is this a stand-alone competitive opportunity, or does it rely on others? Does it support other opportunities? What is the nature of these interdependencies—from increased effectiveness to showstopper?

- *Feasibility.* Are the capabilities needed to capitalize on the competitive opportunity available? What risks are associated with the opportunity? What are the risks associated with the required transformation? How intrusive will the efforts be?

As it turned out, the transition from the bank of today to a bank with a 24/7 self-administered offering and algorithm-based risk management was a big step to think through. The leaders knew that without the capacity and multidisciplinary expertise provided by inclusion, it would not have been possible to holistically detail and evaluate Horizon 1's competitive opportunities.

Sequencing the activities kept the strategic game plan navigable. By consolidating what they had and planning additional journeys for specific horizons, the team members were able to incorporate the work into the bank's ongoing initiatives and start the detailing efforts as part of new initiatives.

C-Bank now had a portfolio of competitive opportunities that had been described and detailed as thoroughly as possible to guide the organization.

Setting Things in Motion: Initiate

The goal of the Initiate stage is to ensure that all initiatives, from minimal housekeeping to the highly strategic, are aimed at the same competitive opportunities and optimally reinforce each other. To ensure action, competitive opportunities must be linked to appropriate initiatives. Like most large organizations, C-Bank was already busy with numerous ongoing initiatives, so the first step was to cross-reference the competitive opportunities with these ongoing initiatives. This revealed which initiatives made sense and should be continued, which ones needed adaptation, which should be stopped, and which areas required new initiatives.

The Initiate stage typically has several outcomes:

- A bottom-up review of current initiatives (ongoing and planned) against the designated competitive opportunities and the strategic game plan, establishing whether these initiatives are:

  - Aligned with and contributing to competitive opportunities

  - Partially aligned with and contributing to competitive opportunities, creating a need to realign the initiatives' objectives

- Not aligned with or even counter to competitive opportunities, creating a need to reconsider the initiative

- A top-down review of competitive opportunities and the strategic game plan to ensure that ongoing and planned initiatives are covered

- Competitive opportunities are monitored as part of ongoing
program management

The main goals here are to ensure (1) that competitive opportunities are reflected in one or more initiatives, and (2) that the opportunities and the game plan are incorporated into program management to
ensure that the implementation is monitored.

Before the project began, C-Bank created a detailed overview of
what was going on in terms of nonroutine improvements and initiatives—both strategic and nonstrategic. It had also terminated or
adapted some of the initiatives that weren't advancing the strategic
game plan or any competitive opportunity.

The leaders had decided earlier, during the Evaluation stage, that
several new initiatives would be needed to capitalize on specific competitive opportunities. Internal IT systems, for example, would require
considerable attention. The amount of transformation involved meant
that everything had to be reviewed, taking into consideration the possibility of acquisitions, partnerships, supplier relationships, and the
development of in-house capabilities. Product development also
required attention, as many of the competitive opportunities relied
heavily on systems capabilities to be cost-effective and feasible.

Once the portfolio of competitive opportunities and the strategic game plan had been developed, all ongoing initiatives were further
evaluated to define what additional initiatives would be necessary to
implement the strategy. The result, interestingly, was not to stop ongoing initiatives and replace them with new and better-aligned initiatives;
rather, many ongoing initiatives were realigned to contribute to the competitive opportunities more directly and, above all, to make these contributions in a mutually reinforcing manner, saving time and resources.

Because C-Bank had a large number of ongoing activities, mostly to address regulatory and IT system changes, it had a relatively well-established program management function that carried out general reporting, including the progress of the bank's major initiatives. However, when the competitive opportunities portfolio was brought into program management to track its progress, the bank discovered that many initiatives were making or should be making concerted contributions to similar competitive opportunities. This had never been acknowledged in C-Bank's program management and reporting.

The New Normal: Embed

Turning a portfolio of competitive opportunities into an element of program management and reporting requires more than a new approach to solving strategic puzzles. It requires new ways of managing strategy and new ways of working. The following are a few requirements that are worth considering from a strategy management perspective:

Strategy cycle. Adapt the strategy cycle to include the three layers: the strategic game plan, the portfolio of competitive opportunities, and the initiatives, especially:

- *Fundamental trends.* Monitor the development of fundamental trends, identifying new trends, assessing their implications, and adapting the overall strategic game plan if required.

- *Competitive opportunities.* Monitor the development of the portfolio of competitive opportunities, tracking the progress of individual opportunities in relation to competitors, adjusting the portfolio if required, and managing the life cycles of opportunities.

- *Program management.* Make the portfolio of competitive opportunities and the strategic initiatives part of the corporate program management effort. This way, each initiative's contributions can be measured against each competitive opportunity and the entire portfolio.

- *Strategic feedback.* Create a learning feedback loop—from the initiatives to the portfolio of competitive opportunities, and from the portfolio to the strategic game plan. Active maintenance enforces this feedback loop, preventing initiatives—strategic or otherwise—from either becoming goals in themselves or just fading away.

Strategic guidance. Reinforce the ability to guide the organization and strengthen a shared sense of purpose.

- *Internal leadership communication.* Incorporate the overall strategic game plan into internal communications by and on behalf of the leadership.

- *Strategy function and business leadership.* Strengthen the company's inspirational capabilities, confidence, and abductive reasoning when evaluating the fundamental trends and competitive opportunities.

- *Governance.* Pass on decision making gradually and where appropriate within the context of stronger, more effective, and more measurable strategic guidance.

Human capital. Draw on contributions from individuals based on their interests and capabilities; these fall outside the confines of job profiles, departments, hierarchy, geographies, or tenures. If strategy is to be turned into an ongoing inclusive activity, contributions must become a continuing aspect of the organization's work.

- *Recognition.* Turn people's enthusiasm for participating into new ways of working through formal recognition—for example, in performance appraisals.

- *Availability.* Acknowledge the need for inclusive efforts and give people room to participate. If inclusive approaches to resolve issues or capture opportunities become more common, this will require more formal accommodation—for example, in budgets.

- *HR processes and policies.* Rethink various HR processes and policies, including career development and strategic resource management, to bring people in from across departments, the hierarchy, and tenures.

Enablement. Inclusive approaches provide substantial resourcing freedom and optimization (getting the right knowledge and experience at the front) but will often rely on complementary technology-related ways of working across organizational, geographic, and time boundaries.

- *Technology.* Most companies already have some collaborative and social technologies in place, but such technologies must be readily available and easy to use.

- *Collaborative skills.* If these are not already in place, the organization must learn technology-enabled, collaborative ways of working. Inclusive approaches can help within a learning-by-doing environment.

Strategy function. There will always be a need for top-down, secretive strategy—for example, in mergers and acquisitions—which means additional requirements and roles for the strategy function.

- Challenge the leaders and the business concerning what is coming their way in terms of fundamental trends.

- Manage the content of the strategic journey.

- Support the evaluation of the competitive opportunities with focused analyses and business plan development.

- Provide moderation and facilitation support in designing and managing organizational inclusiveness and the strategic game plan.

While this list is a long one, remember that many of these activities are determined and developed within a learning-by-doing environment. At the same time, many of them are vital, especially in light of deeply ingrained traditional ways of working. Just as the leaders will need conviction to guide the organization in its strategy formulation, they will also have to strive for the new normal in strategy management—where true inclusion might be the biggest leap of all.

CHAPTER 5

Transformational Strategy

The easiest way to predict the future is to invent it.

—ALAN KAY[1]

I N A DYNAMIC BUSINESS ENVIRONMENT, strategy entails change. Some established firms cope with change by continuing the practices that have made them successful in the past, but finding ways to do things better. Their hope is that better performance will allow them to grab market share and grow the business as the sector expands or, if the sector is stagnant or in decline, at least help the firm survive as the last one standing.

However, as change in the marketplace becomes faster and larger and as the size and shape of the playing field continue to morph in unexpected ways, the chances of winning in a sustainable way merely by doing "more of the same, but better" are declining.

In this chapter, we explore the possibilities of a transformational strategy that grows the playing field, adding new value for customers, capturing the lion's share of an expanding market, and in the process, being disproportionately rewarded. The very uncertainties that characterize the current business environment create huge opportunities for big-win investments that often hide amid uncertainty.

Striking examples of now-famous firms that have succeeded with transformational strategies include Nintendo (as discussed in the Introduction), Amazon, Salesforce, Whole Foods, Walmart, Facebook, Twitter, and Netflix. Amazon transformed first the book business and then all forms of retail and opened up the markets for e-readers and cloud computing. Salesforce transformed customer relationship marketing. Whole Foods changed the notion of what a grocery store could be. Facebook and Twitter transformed the world of social interaction. Netflix altered the way people watch television shows and movies at home.

But transformational strategy is tricky. One retrospective study concluded that the failure rate for established firms was 87 percent.[2] The record for startups is no better. The problem, of course, is anticipating what will delight customers. If you build it, will customers buy it and like it enough to tell their friends about it? Customers themselves can't always predict what they will do. A deep understanding of their wants and needs—and clever design thinking—can help, but this is the probabilistic world of abductive reasoning, continuous experimentation, and rapid learning—not proof.

The delivery side of transformational strategy is particularly fraught with difficulty for established firms. Many of them will need to make changes in the assumptions, attitudes, habits, values, and practices that have made them successful. The more longstanding and fundamental these elements are, and the more successful the company has been, the more effort it will take to change them.

In a recent study, we found that 39 percent of executives and senior managers believe that the responsibility for strategic failure is shared equally by poor strategy formulation and failed deployment. Almost a third believe that both are to blame, but deployment somewhat more, and almost a fifth say that it is the other way around. A very small percentage—6 percent and 7 percent, respectively—point to formulation alone or deployment alone as the reason for failed strategies.

Transformational strategy requires two things. The strategy has to be formulated in such a way that it transcends any combination of assumptions, attitudes, values, habits, and practices—or beliefs—

that might interfere with creating new value for customers in a way that expands the playing field. The strategy also has to generate the assumptions, attitudes, habits, and practices needed to bring it to life. Thus, FutureProof strategy is not an academic, abstract conceptual exercise. Unless the hearts and minds of people in the organization are in sync with the strategy, it will be stillborn.

This is why the principles of future-in (inspiration) and organizational inclusiveness are so important: they help ensure that the process of strategy creation begins the process of creating and reinforcing appropriate assumptions, attitudes, and values that will be the foundation for implementing the strategy.

There are challenges for both established firms and startups. Established firms face a double transformative challenge: toward the market and toward their own ingrained assumptions, attitudes, values, habits, and practices. Startups, on the other hand, do not really face a transformational challenge—they simply have to hire people with the appropriate characteristics to create new value for customers and to extend the playing field. The challenges for startups have more to do with funding, getting access to resources, establishing client relationships, and building a market presence and track record that includes a brand identity. This is not easy, which is why startups have a relatively high failure rate.

Amazon, for example, was founded around a set of transformational beliefs. The possibility introduced by the Internet of independently optimizing the assortment of books (and CDs, DVDs, music, e-books, and now almost every product category imaginable) available, along with warehousing, distribution, order handling, and transactions, was the very reason for starting the company. Amazon did not have to transform its beliefs to pursue a transformational strategy—it simply defined them from scratch and hired people to develop them. It helped that Amazon had a strong leader with a clear vision of where he wanted to take the company. This made it easier to attract and bring on board the right people and prime them with the desired mindset. It also helped that Amazon was able to secure a substantial amount of funding during the dot-com bubble, which got it off to a good start that many of its competitors did not have. In fact, during the early 2000s, some of its competitors were forced to make use of Amazon's e-commerce capabilities, with the result that famous bookstore brands such as Borders and Waterstones were sporting "Powered by Amazon" on their e-commerce sites. This set Amazon on a successful path toward a services business model that was able to sell everything from cloud-based IT services to online e-commerce environments to other businesses.

The challenge for established firms is almost the opposite and is much more daunting. They have an existing business (which more often than not risks being cannibalized by the transformational strategy), access to clients, and a market position, but in order to pursue a transformational strategy, they need to change their assumptions, attitudes, values, habits, and practices. This has proved over and over again to be at least as difficult as starting from scratch because genuine transformations have to go beyond repositioning the firm or changing its business practices. People throughout the organization must develop a new perception of reality. They have to adapt or discard at least some of their ingrained—and often subconscious—core assumptions about how their customers, business, markets, and processes work, as well as the attitudes and values that support those assumptions. This isn't easy. How does an organization discard assumptions that it doesn't even know it has? And how does it know which assumptions are no longer in tune with a changed business environment and should therefore be revised or replaced?

For this to happen, people in the organization must go beyond an intellectual understanding of the need to change. They must internalize why some core assumptions are no longer valid and come to believe that a new set of habits, attitudes, and values is needed if the organization is to prosper both now and in the future. Above all, they must start acting according to those beliefs.

This is where the three principles of FutureProof strategy can help. Bringing in the future through fundamental trends challenges ingrained beliefs. Doing so in an organizationally inclusive way allows this to happen on a meaningful scale. And the portfolio approach to competitive opportunities helps to create a steady stream of new belief-consolidating successes.

Shortcuts Don't Change Beliefs

The challenge in dealing with ingrained beliefs is that they are difficult to change. The leaders can't simply tell the organization that some old beliefs have run their course and need to be adapted or even replaced. The only effective way to change ingrained beliefs is by experiencing a shared success—or, better still, a string of shared successes. Whatever the organization was doing to achieve those successes will become part of its values and beliefs. In contrast, traumatic experiences do not help to change beliefs. In fact, they often either make companies double down on their original recipe for success or kill beliefs. However, in the latter case, the beliefs that are killed are not likely to be replaced by anything that is remotely constructive when it comes to becoming successful again.

This creates a chicken-and-egg riddle: How does a company create shared successes to change the organization's beliefs if it needs the changed beliefs in order to create the successes? Or even before that, how do the leaders know that they are furnishing the organization with new and better beliefs if those beliefs are not the result of shared successes?

JCPenney understands this dilemma. For more than 100 years, the retailer has been an American icon, supplying essential items for everyday living.[3] This Texas-based chain of midrange department stores operates in suburban shopping malls in all 50 U.S. states. But by 2011, JCPenney was losing ground to competitors such as Macy's and Kohl's. A group of investors, led by William Ackman of Pershing Square Capital Management, saw an opportunity for transformational strategy and purchased a stake in the company. The investors persuaded the board to appoint the marketing star of retailing at Apple, Ron Johnson, to run the company.

As expected, Johnson set about rapidly implementing a transformational strategy. "In the U.S.," he said when he joined the firm, "the department store has a chance to regain its status as the leader in style, the leader in excitement. It will be a period of true innovation for this company."

His strategy was to "transform JCPenney from a boring store with boring products into a place with the same kind of pizzazz as Apple." It was widely hailed as bold and exciting.

However, Johnson was well aware of the mismatch between his strategy and the existing managers and staff members, the company culture, the product line, and the marketing and sales policies. He removed most of the existing senior managers and installed his own team of executives.

Because the new strategy was imposed from the top down, many people did not understand or agree with the changes. At headquarters, there was a lack of trust in the new executives, who were commuting each week from California and who, as it turned out, were unfamiliar with department store retailing in general and with JCPenney in particular. The decision to substantially scale back the use of sale price promotions, for example, surprised many seasoned employees. They knew that the hunt for bargains was as much, if not more, an addictive pastime for most shoppers as it was a way to save some money.

Customers stopped coming, and sales plummeted. After 17 months, Johnson was fired. Sale price promotion was reintroduced, but the damage had been done. Customers no longer trusted the store and did not return in sufficient quantities for JCPenney to become profitable.

Johnson's efforts failed to transform the ingrained beliefs of JCPenney's staff and failed to create enough successes to change the organization's ingrained assumptions. It didn't even matter whether his strategy was the right strategy—it simply failed to make it into the minds and hearts of the organization.

The Power of Transformational Beliefs

Johnson's headlong rush into transformational strategy contrasts sharply with Steve Jobs's approach when he took over as interim CEO of Apple in September 1997. Apple had become a big, slow-moving bureaucracy churning out a growing number of computer variants in ever-shorter cycles, but failing to satisfy even its most avid fans. Its business had been devastated by Microsoft's Windows 95. At the time of Jobs's return, Apple was two months away from bankruptcy.

Although many observers had expected Jobs to launch a bold transformational strategy of the kind that Johnson launched at JCPenney, Jobs did the opposite. Through a series of deliberate measures, he put Apple back in touch with its ingrained beliefs of almost a decade earlier—which were already transformational. In doing so, he scaled the company back to its Apple II heyday. Jobs did not have to change the organization's ingrained assumptions about how to be a successful computer company. Its earlier successes, especially through the Apple II family of computers and the brand and company identity that it had built around thinking differently, had been so ingrained within the company that even the troubled years had not wiped them out. The ingrained beliefs only needed to be dusted off.

Jobs did not need to establish ambitious revenue or profit goals or indulge in transformational pronouncements about the future. He simply made sure that the company started to enjoy the kinds of successes that would reconfirm its core beliefs and allow it to take them even further. He cut back and simplified in order to climb out of a financial nosedive. But he did not cut indiscriminately; instead, he took the business back to a simplified line of products that had a usefulness that transcended the hardware and were sold through a limited number of outlets.

The first result of the readopted strategic game plan was the iMac G3, introduced in 1998. Produced initially in Bondi blue and later in other colors, it was considered an industrial design classic. And it was successful, selling 800,000 units in the first several months. And with the G3, Apple made a profit for the first time since 1995. Still, for Apple, this was not transformational but was fully in line with the company's hallmark beliefs: very few variants of highly distinctive and useful products sold in huge numbers to enjoy economies of scale.

The first transformational product came in 2001 with the introduction of the iPod, a digital music player that allowed users to carry 1,000 songs in their pockets. It was preceded by a free music management application and followed a couple of years later by an online music store. The iPod's metal design gave it a unique feel, but what made the iPod transformational was its combination with the iTunes music management software and the iTunes Store, where users could purchase and download any song for just 99 cents. The combination of the iPod, iTunes, and the iTunes Store was greater than the sum of the three products: it created an ecosystem that customers loved and never wanted to leave. The fact that Apple made no money on iTunes and only modest revenues through the iTunes Store didn't matter because customers were willing to pay a premium for the iPod hardware, which brought them to the Apple ecosystem in massive numbers.

Apple created a belief-confirming success that helped it move the notion of usefulness for customers from individual products to entire ecosystems of products and services.

The key to Steve Jobs's success was that he didn't look for a transformational challenge. Instead, he realigned the organization with its latent combination of ingrained assumptions, attitudes, values, habits, and practices, which were already transformational in relation to the market. In fact, he took Apple back to the belief system that he had had an important role in creating.

Building on Winning Beliefs

Apple's evolving beliefs helped it become a successful company again, but that doesn't mean that its beliefs are the only right ones. Many organizations that have enjoyed success with transformational strategies have developed their beliefs over time, building them by gradually becoming more successful, and thus allowing the company to develop a more powerful winning combination of ingrained assumptions, attitudes, values, habits, and practices. They did not have these beliefs as a reason for their existence, as Amazon did, but by pushing the transformational boundaries and simultaneously creating successes in the market, they were able to consolidate their new beliefs.

One good example of such a transformational approach is Zara, a Spanish clothing and accessories retailer.[4] "Zara defies most of the current conventional wisdom about how supply chains should be run," the *Harvard Business Review* wrote in 2004. "The company can design, produce, and deliver a new garment and put it on display in its stores worldwide in a mere 15 days. Such a pace is unheard-of in the fashion business, where designers typically spend months planning for the next season in a cycle that can span more than a year."

Zara is the leading brand of Inditex, a global clothing manufacturer and retailer. Headquartered in Spain, Zara manufactures about half of its production in-house, with only a quarter outsourced to Asia. Instead of relying on outside partners, the company manages its own design, warehousing, distribution, and logistics. Rather than driving its factories to maximize output, Zara deliberately leaves extra manufacturing capacity so that it can respond rapidly to unexpected demand.

Instead of producing only the designs it needs, Zara's designers create approximately 40,000 new designs annually, of which 10,000 are selected for production. Instead of excising all redundant labor, Zara runs three parallel but operationally distinct product families with separate design, sales, and procurement and production planning staffs dedicated to the specific needs of each clothing line: women, men, and children. Instead of separating design from manufacturing, designers sit right in the midst of the production process to facilitate communications.

Rather than aiming for economies of scale, Zara manufactures and distributes products in small batches. Retail stores are required to place orders and accept deliveries in rigid cycles. As a result, regular customers know exactly when new deliveries will come, and therefore visit the stores more frequently on those days. Zara has a policy of zero advertising, relying instead on customer delight and word of mouth.

Instead of shipping clothes as cheaply as possible, Zara ships clothes on racks with price tags already attached so that they can be displayed immediately. Zara often beats the high-fashion houses to the market and offers almost the same products, made with less expensive fabric at much lower prices. Zara sometimes leaves large areas of its expensive retail shops empty so that it can respond flexibly to demand. Zara ignores the potential profits to be made from concentrating on its bestselling items, but instead even encourages them to sell out, thus enticing customers to shop more often and more promptly.

Zara's transformational strategy appears to have been inspired by its starting position of having manufacturing capacity in Spain, its fashion-conscious home market. Instead of following other clothing manufacturers down the outsourcing-to-Asia route, Zara sought ways to take advantage of its in-house manufacturing capacity and developed the concept of "instant fashion," which allowed the brand to respond to consumer trends quickly.

The results have been remarkable. Despite the struggling Spanish economy and an industry characterized by mercurial and quixotic customer demand, Zara is flourishing and has helped its parent company, Inditex, become one of the two largest clothing retailers in the world. Because Zara can offer a large variety of the latest designs quickly and in limited quantities, it collects 85 percent of the full ticket price on its retail clothing, while the industry average is 60 to 70 percent.[5]

Zara's example shows that many different belief systems are conducive to extracting value. It's not one size fits all. It also shows that growth can be used to experiment, allow the organization's assumptions to evolve over time, and keep the offering relevant and competitive. To keep the brand alive, Zara was able to balance the need to challenge its organizational beliefs with the need to capitalize on them.

Transformation—One Belief at a Time

A good starting point for identifying competitive opportunities is the company's ingrained assumptions about trade-offs, escalations, dogmas, and bottlenecks. Unearthing these underlying assumptions and challenging them through integrative thinking can help produce a solution that, for example, doesn't require making trade-offs. In fact, you can have both—bypass bottlenecks altogether and find an alternative to staying in an escalating maelstrom of ever better, more comprehensive, and more expensive ways of meeting customer demands.

There are many good examples of companies that have transformed single ingrained assumptions. As mentioned earlier, Nintendo challenged a core assumption of the gaming industry—that a game's graphics quality was crucial to its success. When it introduced the Wii, it was so successful that it was in short supply for years. It took Sony more than eight years to sell more PlayStations than Nintendo sold Wii consoles. In fact, at one point, Nintendo sold more Wii consoles than Microsoft's Xbox and Sony's PlayStation combined.

Walmart's green initiative is another good example. The ingrained wisdom was that going green required an economic trade-off. Ecologically sounder alternatives would be more expensive than their regular counterparts and thus would be too expensive for Walmart's cost-conscious customers. Books such as *The Triple Bottom Line* by John Ellington in 1997 had shown that going green could go hand in hand with direct economic benefits, but this thinking had not yet been adopted by mainstream businesses or, more important for Walmart, the minds of most consumers.

In 2006, Walmart decided to get serious about selling compact fluorescent light (CFL) energy-saving bulbs. The company figured that customers would save around $30 worth of electricity over the life span of the bulb, and if it could sell 100 million CFL bulbs, it would also save the emissions equivalent of about 0.7 million cars on the road, one power generation plant, or the electricity needed for 450,000 single-family homes. The benefits didn't stop there. In addition to benefiting consumers' wallets and the environment, CFL bulbs would bring Walmart substantial economic benefits. For one thing, these bulbs increased the value density of the product category by a factor of 5 to 10 times over the standard incandescent lamp, and this was boosted even further by the 10-times-longer life span of a CFL bulb. This meant that transport costs—and emissions—could be slashed and shelf space could be saved. To top it off, because CFL bulbs were more expensive than incandescent bulbs, the *margin* potential of a CFL bulb was greater than the *revenue* potential of incandescent bulbs.

Walmart sold 100 million CFL bulbs well ahead of schedule and in the process created considerable awareness of these bulbs among consumers. The retailer also created a shared success that helped change an ingrained organizational belief that sustainability costs money to a new belief that sustainability is a genuine and attractive business opportunity. Many companies now look at green as a source of opportunities rather than a trade-off.

Growing Transformational Urgency

These examples from Zara, Nintendo, and Walmart demonstrate that ingrained beliefs are like an embedded strategic compass that guides an organization in most of what it does. This is generally a good thing because it helps align the entire organization and prevents the leaders and managers from having to micromanage. We also learned that deliberate efforts can be made to keep ingrained beliefs current or redirect them toward emerging opportunities, especially if they are consolidated within a steady stream of shared successes. And the actual transformational distance covered by even iconic companies can be fairly modest; Apple simply went back to where it had been before it tried to become a normal computer company and failed, and Amazon continued to do and build on what it had set out to do when it was founded.

It makes sense for established firms to simply make the most of their ingrained assumptions as they work to change them—unless, of course, the firm is facing a faster-changing, more dynamic business environment. In that case, a work-on-it-as-we-go approach can quickly become problematic. When change is coming from multiple directions, sometimes ingrained beliefs must change if the company is to stay in the game—not just to capture new business opportunities.

Things become more complicated when the belief system needs a major overhaul. This leads to the circular challenge of changing an organization's ingrained beliefs in order to create the successes necessary to change those beliefs. This is one reason why game changes and disruptions are often brought about by startups—organizations that are built from scratch around a promising belief system, with little downside if the new system doesn't work out.

Driving Transformational Strategies

Unlike startups, established firms should address their ingrained assumptions and beliefs before they consider a transformational strategy. Here, a FutureProof approach is useful in bringing belief-challenging future inspiration into an organizationally inclusive setting to create a surrogate startup situation. This is especially effective when organizational inclusiveness is broad and self-selected, as this level of participation closely mimics the way a typical startup addresses its most relevant trends.

As the implications of trends become clear and the opportunities become more palpable, the entire organization begins to see its future and its ingrained assumptions in a whole new light. And as participants in the strategy process share their new perceptions of reality with the broader organization, this paves the way for subsequent efforts to capitalize on concrete competitive opportunities and improve day-to-day activities, thus further increasing the chances of genuine belief-shifting experiences.

The Digital Agenda

Technology is a main factor forcing companies to adopt transformational strategies just to stay in the game. The change brought about by advanced technologies can be so profound that it erodes the relevance of belief systems faster than organizations can adapt them.

Companies in a variety of industries—and not just the information-driven ones—must understand the likely impact and opportunities of digital trends, the possible strategic outcomes, and what this all means for their organizational beliefs. Although such knowledge will not safeguard a company from everything that the future will throw at it, the company will stand a better chance of anticipating the changes so to take advantage of them rather than fall victim to them.

Leaders must be open to being challenged and discovering that some of their ingrained assumptions are no longer valid, while also *actively searching* for assumptions and beliefs that have run their course. Changing ingrained beliefs holds the key to true innovation; clinging to them holds a company back.

New Management Practices to Support Strategy

The requirements of transformational strategy are another reason why new practices in strategy require new practices in management. "Traditional management creates profound dis-economies of scale," Nicholas Vitalari and Haydn Shaughnessy say in their 2012 book *The Elastic Enterprise*. "Scale has come to equate with sclerosis because the costs associated with organizing more and more people scale more quickly than the additional wealth those people create."

Apple met the diverse needs of hundreds of millions of iPhone users by launching an ecosystem—a technology platform that enabled hundreds of thousands of developers to create apps that could meet every conceivable human need and then offer those apps directly to customers. The result is a device that is easily adapted to meet the needs, preferences, and passing whims of every user—a feat that is inconceivable with traditional management practices and in-house approaches to meeting every customer's every need.

Strategy formulation is often a joint process of creative discovery with customers and business partners. As value chains become more networked and more like ecosystems, more strategizing across business boundaries and within buyer-supplier relationships will be required. There are already many successful examples, from Procter & Gamble redefining the development function in the fast-moving consumer goods industry to LEGO drawing some of its most cherished customers into product development.

Strategy Is Companywide

The bar has been raised. Strategy needs to be released from the confines of the C-suite and made truly inclusive. The knowledge and expertise of people in different parts of the organization can collectively decipher the recipes for capturing value and their specific contributions. Without an understanding of what the individual parts are capable of, strategy is difficult to formulate.

At the same time, implementation suffers if parts of the company do not know how they fit in, both now and in the future. A portfolio approach to managing competitive opportunities and strategic initiatives within the strategic game plan helps to ensure that competitive opportunities see the light of day.

FutureProof strategy begins with future *inspiration* to better understand the fundamental trends that could be decisive for the company. Assessing the implications of such trends helps leaders rethink at least some of their ingrained beliefs, while *inclusiveness* is a powerful principle to help larger parts of the organization reconsider their own beliefs while getting a heads-up on what the future looks like. The choice of trends is crucial; this is how the leadership sets the strategic direction.

Transformational strategy is about expanding the playing field. But strategy must also address the possibility that the playing field may be contracting in unexpected ways as a result of disruption or other competitive threats. It is to these issues that we now turn.

CHAPTER 6

Dealing with Disruption and Competitive Threats

Keep an eye on the vulture—while you are hard at work, he is circling above.

—Robert Greene[1]

In Chapter 5, we explored stepping out of the shadows of ingrained beliefs to grasp strategic opportunities. But business is not just about opportunities. Businesses must be aware of and deal with shifting competitive threats, unexpected contractions of the playing field, and major shifts among players—what is commonly referred to as *disruptive innovation*.

In principle, the inspirational, inclusive, and portfolio processes described in earlier chapters can be used equally well to pursue growth opportunities and to deal with market contractions and disruptions. However, the dynamics are very different. When we are pursuing competitive opportunities, we do not have to see all of them with perfect long-term vision—just enough of them to secure an attractive future. Yet, when it comes to threats and disruptions, even those that we do not see can harbor our downfall.

Getting the future right matters more when it comes to threats and disruptions than it does for opportunities. But strategy is an art and not an exact science, so no one expects to get it 100 percent right. Getting the future even 80 percent right is a considerable accomplishment.

In this chapter, we address the 20 percent of unforeseen possibilities that constitute the "friction" and the "fog of war" that accompany strategy in changing times and how to minimize them.

The Dark Side of Threats and Disruption

In Chapter 5, we discussed the point that in principle, transformational strategies are much simpler for startups than for existing businesses because startups do not have to change their assumptions, attitudes, habits, values, and practices—their entire belief systems—the way existing businesses do. Startups can simply hire people into a belief system that was set up specifically to create new values and extend the playing field. In addition, it is acceptable if a startup fails outright or doesn't become a shining success. In fact, we expect only a very small number of startups to become the next Facebook or Amazon. Existing businesses do not have this luxury. The economic and social costs of failure for an existing and previously successful business are perceived to be much higher, so failure is not really an option.

Existing businesses, especially the sizable ones with successful histories that span decades, are at even more of a disadvantage when it comes to threats and disruptions than they are with opportunities. In fact, the stronger the company's ingrained beliefs, know-how, past successes, and assumptions, the more risk it runs of not discerning threats or properly assessing their severity until it is too late. This sets them up to be disrupted—by startups created specifically for that purpose.

Sometimes You Really Can't Win

There is something even more disturbing about threats and disruption: things could actually get worse. Imagine this situation: There is no threat that can be staved off or disruption that can be avoided.

There is only a less attractive future ahead that can at best be delayed or adjusted to. The company sees the threat or disruption coming, but it doesn't matter what it does to try to avoid, mitigate, or accommodate it. The disruption will hit. The company can influence only the degree of the disruption.

There are many well-documented examples of companies that have faced such prospects. Kodak knew perfectly well that digital photography would hurt its film business. It had even invented the core technologies for digital photography. Many people accuse Kodak of fumbling the transition to digital, which eventually led to its filing for Chapter 11 in early 2012. But in reality, with a 90 percent market share in North America alone, Kodak did not have much to gain by making the transition from being one of two highly profitable, globally dominant photographic film players to becoming one of many electronics firms producing digital cameras, technologies, or memory cards in a highly competitive, crowded market. Now more pictures are taken with iPhones than with any other camera, which shows the extent of the dynamics faced by digital photography players.

Lighting companies that produced magnetic ballasts for fluorescent lighting faced a similar situation a decade ago. Life was good. They operated in a global market that had only a few players, and they enjoyed the scale advantages of a highly specialized and mechanical production process. Then came electronic ballasts—lighter, cheaper, environmentally friendlier, and with more ways to control lighting conditions. Existing players suddenly had to compete with a large number of electronics manufacturers in a business with a lower price point and lower margins. Not even the volumes resulting from a regulatory-driven transition to electronic ballasts could make up for the lost margins—even if these companies had held on to their market share.

Getting the Most out of Disruption

The fact that things can get worse is not a reason to become complacent. Instead, it provides a good reason to understand how a

FutureProof strategy can help a company avoid surprises that make threats or disruptions even worse and, if possible, allow it to survive in the best possible shape.

Charles Schwab, the discount broker turned financial services provider, astutely introduced online brokerage in 1996, knowing full well that the online price levels would be a threat to its already competitively priced phone-based brokerage business. Schwab counted on the expectation that the online brokerage business would eventually become a much larger, albeit lower-margin, business. As a discount broker, it could not pass up the opportunity.

Or consider Adobe, the U.S.-based maker of Photoshop and other professional graphics software. Software businesses in general face a number of big fundamental trends, including that more software is now available from the cloud. Adobe is actively dealing with this trend. Despite five quarters of declining earnings (on a year-to-year basis), Adobe's share price was flying high in the summer of 2014, compared to a year earlier and compared to the S&P 500.[2]

According to the *Economist*, Adobe "has defied gravity because investors are bullish about the dramatic shift that the firm is making from being a purveyor of pricey, shrink-wrapped software to one that charges users a monthly subscription fee to access its applications online via the computing 'cloud'—vast warehouses of servers run by Adobe and other firms. Like the music industry, Adobe is abandoning selling its wares on physical discs to rent them out online."[3]

The *Economist* praised Adobe for having the courage to change its business model in real time.

> The transformation of its business model has been pretty drastic. . . . Instead of forking out up to $2,600 for Creative Suite, its flagship design package on a disc, customers can now use its Creative Cloud service, which offers the same applications (plus a few additional ones) online, with a 12-month subscription costing $50 a month, or a month-by-month fee of $75. This has caused Adobe's profits to crater in the short term, but investors are betting that they will

rebound over time, as the subscription model attracts many new customers who had balked at the prices of its packaged software.[4]

"Wall Street isn't entirely stupid," said strategy consultant and business professor Roger Martin.

If a cogent argument is made for a different business model, then it will listen. Most such company arguments lack cogency, and that's why they fall on entirely deaf ears. This is particularly interesting because it has long been thought that a traditional license-selling software company can't cross the chasm into a software-as-a-service model because the transitional hit on revenues is just too brutal. Once you get to the other side, it is great and arguably a superior model with a recurring revenue base. But it is brutal to build up that base. It's important for Adobe to succeed because it will help Wall Street understand that it is doable. Others will then follow.[5]

Identifying Potential Threats and Disruptions

Minimizing the impact of threats and disruptions requires first understanding the possible impact of fundamental trends that affect the business—the kind that could cause a major shift among players or in the market.

Since Clayton Christensen introduced the world to "disruptive innovation" in his 1997 book *The Innovator's Dilemma*, there is the notion that any business can be disrupted in a flash and that companies need to become disruptors if they don't want to become victims. However, a look into some of the more notorious disruption cases of the past couple of decades shows that while many of these disruptions were spectacular in their outcomes, they were in the making for a long time—enough time for companies to figure out what was going on had they made a serious effort to investigate. (Also, not all disrupted companies were disrupted out of existence. Many actually survived and thrived after navigating the disruption.)

Apple, for example, had immense success with the iPad, which took the market by storm in 2010. The iPad created a new market segment, sold in incredible numbers in a short period of time, and even had an impact on laptop sales. Yet it cannot be called a real surprise. In speeches as far back as 1983, Steve Jobs talked about a computer in a book that would exchange information through radio signals. This makes the beginnings of this high-speed disruption look like a slow-moving ramp-up, or even a failed experiment.

Think back to the early 1980s and personal digital assistants (PDAs). The market was led by the Psion 1, followed in the early 1990s by HP's 95LX, Psion's Series 3, Nokia's Communicator, Apple's Newton, U.S. Robotics' PalmPilot and later Palm V, HP's iPAQ, and RIM's range of BlackBerries. All this time, the notion of a relatively small, easy-to-carry, smart electronic device held promise, and many companies pursued its potential. Apple, for one, had ambitious goals for the Newton, aiming to reinvent personal computing and rewrite application programming. But the Newton project fell victim to project slippage, scope creep, and a growing fear that it would cannibalize Macintosh sales. So it was reinvented as a complement to the Macintosh instead of a stand-alone computer. According to former Apple CEO John Sculley, the corporation invested about $100 million to develop the Newton.[6] But in each incarnation, it was unsuccessful in the marketplace and failed to convince customers.

Creating an inflection point took several technological trends becoming strong simultaneously in the latter half of the 2000s. As devices continued to become exponentially more useful, combined with growing mobile connectivity, the network effect in application development, and user communities, PDAs became a huge success as smartphones, e-readers, and tablets sold in the tens of millions, all in a few years. And now the iPhone, the most successful smartphone, has become the most used digital camera in the world, going well beyond the early anticipated use of the small personal electronic device.

Another example is Google Maps and other app-based navigation solutions that stopped the growth of the physical navigation device market dead in its tracks and pushed it into decline with little hope of recovery. The big bang that occurred in 2011 was a while in the making. The first smartphone with GPS and maps appeared in 1999. It was a slow-moving, clumsy affair, but that was bound to change as the underlying fundamental trends moved forward. The power of computers was improving exponentially in accordance with Moore's law (screens, GPS accuracy, download speeds, energy consumption, battery size, and so on).[7] Similar improving trends were visible in connectivity from 1995 onward. Steadily growing smartphone coverage exploded with the 2007 success of Apple's iPhone. Entertainment and information in cars was steadily moving from luxury vehicles to all midsized cars. Moreover, the makers of physical GPS devices were steadily making greater use of the Internet to upgrade the capabilities of their devices. The flow of information globally was accelerating at marginal cost to users as Google moved forward with its goal of "organizing the world's information."

A review of these trends would have revealed that the development of a ubiquitous, free online navigation solution and the disruption of the market for physical navigation devices were only a matter of time. What wasn't clear was which firm would be the one to do this and when. It turned out to be Google in 2011. Google Maps is the world's most popular smartphone app, with more than 54 percent of global smartphone owners using it at least once during August 2013.[8] Apple's effort to duplicate Google's feat was flawed and resulted in an apology from Apple CEO Tim Cook for having released a product that didn't meet Apple's high standards.

Organization on the Lookout

FutureProof strategy provides help on two fronts for identifying threats and potential disruptions. First of all, the approach is anchored in exploring and understanding fundamental trends and ranking them on their speed of change and their relative importance to the company. This provides an ideal starting point for using the trends to screen for potential threats and disruptions, especially by looking into the ways in which they might reinforce each other and create inflection points.

The second front is scenario planning, which is useful in bringing together the known trends and the unknown trends. Scenarios are advantageous in testing the output of strategic efforts, raising awareness about future uncertainty and thus increasing the organization's ability to be on the lookout. When strategy is turned into an inclusive and ongoing affair, threats and potential disruptions are monitored from all corners of the organization, especially when the possible inflection points are articulated up front.

Clayton Christensen also showed in *The Innovator's Dilemma* that the biggest challenge facing businesses when they are dealing with threats and potential disruptions is their existing business and the profits it makes. This works like a straitjacket, keeping the firm focused on continually improving its existing business instead of looking further ahead at looming or even imminent disruptions. In other words, the problem is not the difficulty of seeing the threat or disruption; it is the difficulty of acting on such insights.

Dealing with Distractions

Distractions can prevent companies from seeing the changes that are heading their way and identifying the most likely courses of action. Stock markets, for example, can be a distraction for public companies. Quarterly numbers expectations, shareholder value, and takeovers—especially in the absence of a powerful guiding competitive strategy—can become goals in themselves and frustrate efforts to look at the future with a broader perspective.

The global financial and economic crisis following the 2008 collapse of Lehman Brothers was a major distraction. Being forced to adapt to a new and much less attractive market reality forced companies to think and act in the here and now at the expense of increasing their advantage in the future and even relative to customers and competitors. Similarly, the past decade has made it abundantly clear that a socially and environmentally conscious way of doing business has become the new norm. For many companies, this has meant profound changes in the way they operate—so much so that the distinction between efforts to adapt to this new reality and efforts to create superior customer value and advantaged delivery to outperform others can become blurred.

Setting Up for Disruption

In addition to dealing with distractions, leaders also have to ensure that their organization is prepared to embrace the disruptive innovation and compete with the potential disruptors head on. The difficulty with this is that, as Clayton Christensen and Michael Raynor's book *The Innovator's Solution* points out, organizations tend to crush disruptive new ideas because they represent a threat to management, careers, power structures, customary ways of thinking, client bases, brands, corporate culture, and profits. Christensen and Raynor therefore suggest protecting the disruptive new business from these hostile forces by creating an independent organizational unit where the innovation can flourish without having to fight off the interferences and anti-innovation attitudes of the existing culture.

The pros and cons of this separate setup are the subject of much debate. Despite its attractiveness, it has several disadvantages. An independent unit can't address innovations that require organization-wide change and may have difficulty getting the resources necessary for success. After all, as Christensen and Raynor point out, the parent organization doesn't really want the innovation to succeed, and even if the independent unit is successful, the firm still faces the issue of what happens next. In theory, the parent company should embrace the unit's success, but in practice, it often folds the subsidiary into the mainstream of the organization and crushes it to death, as happened with the PC division of IBM and the Saturn division of General Motors. That's because the attitudes, values, and practices of the new business were incompatible with those of the parent firm.

Most important, however, when dealing with disruptive innovation that will ultimately affect the entire organization, protecting innovation in a separate unit still leaves open the question about when to change the broader organization. Anchoring the innovation in a separate unit only delays dealing with the issue of what to do with the core business, and it reduces the amount of time available to deal with this issue. This lost time might be needed for the mindset change that is required if the company is to turn the disrupted core business into an organization that is able to take advantage of at least some of the changing circumstances and able to fight off the disruptors. This is likely to require all the time available.

In such situations, a FutureProof strategy can help the organizational mindset change and the transformation progress. Instead of protecting the innovation in a separate setup, the entire organization's appreciation for the innovation can be captured right from the start. By engaging a sufficiently large part of the organization in dealing with the most important fundamental trends, both awareness and ownership are created to deal with the implications, including possible disruptions. This helps in two ways. First, engaging the organization in formulating a response to a potential threat or disruption reduces the need for or time required to go through a sequential process. And, more important, it draws on the organization's full resourcefulness, which can help give it and the leadership the confidence to tackle the threat or disruption head on and improve the chances of coming out on top.

Getting Started

*Every case is unique. It is all a matter of seeing through
the fog of uncertainty in which every situation is
shrouded, making an accurate assessment of what
you do know, guessing what you do not know,
reaching a conclusion rapidly and then vigorously and
unwaveringly following it through.*

—HELMUTH VON MOLTKE[1]

WE HAVE DISCUSSED HOW RECLAIMING strategy as the overriding management system and applying three principles—drawing inspiration from the future, involving the organization, and taking a portfolio approach—can transform strategy into powerful organizational energy. But the world is a complex place, and FutureProof strategy is not a silver bullet.

In this chapter, we discuss how to get started with FutureProof strategy, how to avoid some common pitfalls, and how to manage the risks.

Aim at FutureProof Strategy's Sweet Spot

When an organization is operating in a fast-changing business environment, swamped by attempts to respond and adapt, while at the

155

same time being prevented from formulating effective and enduring responses, a solid strategy can provide a lifeline.

FutureProof strategy draws on the collective knowledge and expertise of the organization to translate fundamental trends into relevant opportunities for creating competitive advantage, and turning strategy into a continuing guiding force.

This, of course, is not the ideal approach in situations that do not directly involve the organization, such as confidential mergers and acquisitions, corporate portfolio strategies, financing strategies, or strategies that negatively affect people through downsizing. In these situations, constructive organizational inclusiveness will be difficult to achieve.

Begin with a Mindset Change

FutureProof strategy is a departure from traditional large-scale analysis-driven approaches. It requires more than just following the steps in a recipe. It requires rethinking commonly held beliefs about strategy.

When companies are rolling out traditional strategies, a primary obstacle is that people cannot or will not change their ingrained beliefs upon orders from above, or upon instructions to embrace a new future. The bleak reality is that major transformation efforts have an abysmal 30 percent success rate.[2] The new way forward can be communicated, but the convictions needed to drive its implementation cannot be handed down.

Our approach resolves this by including major parts of, and sometimes all of, the organization in the strategy formulation process. People are exposed to the fundamental trends that are most likely to affect the organization's future, and this helps to create awareness about what's expected to be coming in the future. Then, using the collective knowledge and experience of the organization, the trends are turned into opportunities for capturing competitive advantage. The organization experiences the next best thing to shared success: a jointly charted path to a prosperous future and shared ownership of the journey ahead.

Purpose Is Not What's on Paper, but What's Accomplished

In confusing times, having a clear guiding purpose is reassuring. It is no surprise that many organizations work hard to strengthen their shared sense of purpose. And the stakes have been raised: having a common purpose is a key motivator for knowledge workers, who make up a large part of today's organizations. But just like new mind-sets, a sense of purpose cannot be taught. And while it is helpful to get the desired purpose down on paper, or on the obligatory 3 × 5 laminated cards, doing so does not bring it to life. Purpose lives in what we do. The strategic approach outlined in the previous chapters can make powerful contributions to reestablishing a common sense of purpose by pulling people together to work on things that truly matter for the future and for what the organization aims to be.

From Insights Through Analyses to Analyses of Insights

The value of analysis-driven strategies goes only so far in a rapidly changing business environment. Data, after all, favor the present over the future and the known over the unknown, which is exactly the opposite of what is required to develop a strategy in uncertain, dynamic environments. Our approach reverses the role of analysis. Instead of using analysis to develop strategic insights, the focus is on identifying the most important fundamental trends and their implications. Analysis is then used to evaluate, quantify, and validate these insights to provide decision-making support.

Unpredictability Is Caused by Predictable Trends

Fundamental trends are at the core of a FutureProof strategy. They play out over decades rather than years, are directionally predictable, and have a profound impact. But when several trends are affecting business environments simultaneously, the combined effect can be both unpredictable and disruptive. When people understand the most important trends and assess their implications and the opportunities to create competitive advantage, strategy becomes manageable again.

Decide What Should Be Proven, Not What Can Be Proven

Running a business comes with considerable responsibility, and especially in larger businesses, decisions are expected to be based solely on well-substantiated information. Yet in a faster and more profoundly changing environment, making decisions based only on what can be proven to be advantageous can be a severely limiting factor. Think about all the unprovable but attractive opportunities that you've missed.

FutureProof strategy resolves this by combining two tactics. First, the approach doesn't work deterministically through inductive or deductive logic. It works probabilistically with questions of abductive logic: Might this become true? How likely is it to become true? What would follow if it did become true? What things would have to happen for it to become true? How feasible are those things?

Second, the strategy emphasizes experimentation to prove that competitive opportunities are worthy of pursuit. Creating a link between the game plan, the portfolio of competitive opportunities, and the strategic initiatives allows for continual, ongoing feedback learned "on the ground" from those deploying the strategic initiatives.

Inclusiveness Represents More Control

Strategy that cascades from the top down gives the appearance of control. However, this can be deceptive. Even if the strategy proves to be right and even if the leaders are able to translate the strategy into plans and detailed instructions, there is still a formidable change management hurdle to get over to turn people into true believers.

FutureProof strategy increases control by inviting the organization into the strategy formulation process. Large parts of the organization are turned into ambassadors for the strategic game plan, which they take beyond their formulation and deployment duties into their day-to-day activities. At the same time, more people are aware of and anticipate the changes that are coming their way, which leads to a more coordinated organization.

Leaders maintain control over the process by selecting the fundamental trends and determining how the company intends to take advantage of them. This provides a strong direction for all strategy formulation efforts. The leaders also determine the game plan for the journey. And by introducing a portfolio of competitive opportunities—each with its own strategic approach—it is possible to control the outcome.

A NEW CEO TAKES A FUTUREPROOF APPROACH

The first day on a new job is never easy. J.G. knew that his challenges were going to be difficult. But he was prepared. This was his fourth time at bat as CEO of a major retailer. This retailer, much like the others, needed an organization-wide transformation. J.G. had a 3-0 record of successful turnarounds. He often joked that he was this generation's "Chainsaw Al" Dunlap. But that was just talk. In truth, J.G. had a knack for thoughtful rather than slash-and-burn tactics.

Within six months, J.G. reached out to us for assistance. He now had a handle on the challenges, and he was ready for in-depth discussions of the retailer's current situation and future prospects. The people on the management team, he explained, had been focused almost exclusively on the financials—they were preoccupied with same-store revenue growth, margin per store area, and optimal use of shelf space. In the past two years, the retailer had lost touch with its customers, and in an interesting turn, the entire organization had lost touch with the company's roots and its traditional pride. The retailer had a solid history and a trusted reputation, but it was not keeping up with the numerous new ways to attract customers. In fact, e-commerce and digital services were nowhere on its radar. J.G. understood that customers would be loyal only up to a point. Eventually, convenience would win out over loyalty.

When we arrived for our first meeting with the management team, J.G. wasted no time in getting to the point: "It is clear that we need a new strategy, something that really helps us take advantage of the changes that are coming our way," he began. "But simply coming up with a strategy will not be enough because our people are not in the right frame of mind to do something with it. These folks are burned out. There have been too many starts and stops over the past few years, so people don't trust management enough to throw themselves into another major strategy project. Plus, we have to make changes now—literally *now*—or this place is going under."

When a workforce has lost confidence and no longer cares whether or not the company succeeds, launching a strategy from the top down is not the right approach. Instead, the best approach is to merge strategy development with change management. "Engaging large parts of the organization in the strategy effort is essential to achieving full awareness of the company's situation—in this case a dire one," we explained to the management team. "Organizational inclusiveness is the best way to get to the heart of market trends, to understand what customers' needs are now, and to predict what those needs are likely to be in the future."

With an inclusive approach, the entire organization becomes the driving force for change. Everyone is involved in rediscovering the firm's mission and in restoring a sense of purpose. Rather than simply solving a strategic puzzle, the solutions to the puzzle are shared and fully owned by the entire organization.

We added that while involving key people in strategy development takes more time in the beginning (compared to a traditional strategy project), this time is quickly made up during deployment. This is because change management is incorporated into the rollout, and therefore there is less risk of a failed rollout. "We essentially combine strategy and change into a strategic journey."

To get the ball rolling, we confronted the organization with a long list of its ongoing business improvement initiatives, outlining which ones made strategic sense and which ones were questionable and could be eliminated. "This exercise provided our first sense of shared achievement," J.G. said. "By eliminating projects and efforts that would make questionable contributions to our business success, we freed up time to devote to launching this new strategy effort."

Our team then engaged the organization in several sources of strategic inspiration:

- *Strategic audits.* These were carried out to demonstrate the retailer's true competitive position and highlight several acute threats, including the way large players like Walmart and a handful of online upstarts had managed to encroach on the retailer's turf. Both would have to be dealt with.

- *Scenario-planning workshops.* These were aimed at identifying the fundamental trends that would affect the retailer and the trends that would affect its customers. A deeper dive into the trends affecting customers highlighted the need to launch digital and online services.

- *Assessments of customer needs.* This was done to enable the company to reconnect with today's customers while gaining insights into how to serve customers in the years ahead.

In addition, key members of the organization participated in "ideation" sessions to identify and filter potential growth opportunities. These sessions allowed for more awareness of where and how to pursue the most attractive and achievable growth opportunities. And they helped people fully internalize the reasons why. Instead of being presented with outcomes, people fully understood why the pursuit of growth was necessary for the company's very survival.

Several other aspects of this process helped in the transformation. For example, initiating an inclusive business plan development process meant that the organization fully owned the decisions and their outcomes.

Finally, and perhaps most important, the strategy effort helped to reestablish the company's purpose. "It served the additional function of separating our people from their ingrained perceptions," J.G. said in summarizing the successes. "The effort helped all of us—the entire organization—become reacquainted with our customers."

From Multiyear Cycles to Ongoing Strategic Guidance

One of the most notable differences between large-scale analysis-driven strategy efforts and FutureProof strategy is the ability to provide continual, ongoing management. Rather than using a sequential process of formulation and deployment, it is possible to combine clear strategic direction with agility, thereby continually adjusting the strategy based on firsthand, on-the-ground experience. The portfolio of competitive opportunities provides a bridge between a long-term strategic game plan and the here-and-now initiatives that make strategy happen (see Figure 7.1).

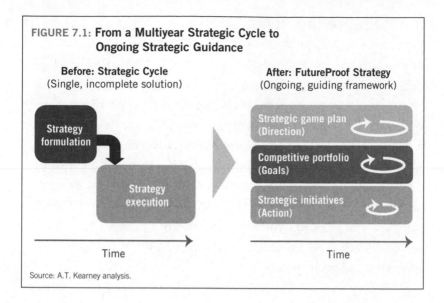

FIGURE 7.1: **From a Multiyear Strategic Cycle to Ongoing Strategic Guidance**

Before: Strategic Cycle
(Single, incomplete solution)

After: FutureProof Strategy
(Ongoing, guiding framework)

Strategy formulation

Strategy execution

Strategic game plan (Direction)

Competitive portfolio (Goals)

Strategic initiatives (Action)

Time

Time

Source: A.T. Kearney analysis.

From Strategic Specialists to Strategic Tour Guides

Strategy teams are often made up of strategic planning specialists, M&A experts, market and competitive analysis professionals, business planners, and other highly skilled and competent people who can solve almost any strategic puzzle. But intellect does not equate to making strategy happen and enjoying the advantages that strategic solutions can bring.

The strategic focus must shift from solving the puzzle to implementing the solution—and this requires changing the way in which the puzzle is solved. Rather than being handed over to the specialists and leaders, strategy becomes organizationally inclusive. People with firsthand knowledge and experience are brought into the process, and most important, they are brought in right from the start, when the strategy is being formulated. The specialists and leaders, who are typically most comfortable with being the brains behind the strategy, must now also guide the strategic journey.

Don't Ignore the Risks

Traditional top-down strategy is relatively risk free. When leaders decide that a strategy is no longer working, they simply form a new one. Cynics would argue that this doesn't really matter, since most strategies aren't fully implemented anyway. FutureProof strategy is different. Once larger parts of the organization are engaged in creating the strategy, it can no longer be stopped at will if the direction that is emerging doesn't suit the leaders—even if their reasons are perfectly valid. Changing directions is likely to lead to irreparable disillusionment and growing cynicism. FutureProof strategy is certainly not without its risks, but the risks are acknowledged and therefore can be addressed and mitigated.

Don't Fail to Lead

If people are invited into the strategy formulation process but do not receive guidance, their contributions tend to be broad. Contributions that are spread too thin fail to get to the heart of the matter, and many are not used. As a result, participants are often disappointed and disillusioned and are less likely to remain interested in the process.

The remedy for this is leaders who are confident about the overall direction in which the company is headed and well versed in the game plan. The best leaders are those who stand in front of the organization and point in the right direction, then ask for help in figuring out how to get there.

Because FutureProof strategy is aspirational and inspirational, leaders must be able to provide the organization with a convincing perspective on how to take advantage of change. This might require leaders to do some old-fashioned soul-searching to challenge their own assumptions and ingrained beliefs before they can get ahead of the organization and lead.

Don't Be Tempted by Quick Wins

When companies have a lot on their plate, it is tempting to pursue quick wins to get things moving in the right direction. But quick wins alone are not conducive to a durable winning culture. They focus the organization on transactional, short-term goals; from there, it is difficult to make the transition to a longer-term strategic mindset. Ideally, quick wins are positioned within the context of a longer-term strategy. This way, the shared successes confirm the overall direction and help lay the foundation for growing advantage.

Don't Think That Secrecy Makes Strategies Stronger

Many people believe that strategy should be formulated in secret so that it can't be copied and so that competitors will be caught off guard. This is understandable, and it would be a good idea if strategy could be achieved with the flip of a switch. But it can't. Organizations have to move mountains to get ambitious strategies implemented. Strategic advantage comes not from *having* the strategy but from *doing* the strategy, and this means that people throughout the organization need to know what the strategy is. And the sooner they know it, the better. Engaging people early in formulating strategy leads to a more and better informed organization, which leads to strategies being put in place sooner, which leads to surprised competitors. In other words, the sooner the organization knows what the strategy is, the greater the chances for success.

Above All, Don't Fake Inclusion

It is tempting to see organizational inclusiveness as a tool to create buy-in. In reality, it is almost the opposite. People know instantly when an invitation to the "party" is not sincere and was set up only to create buy-in for preconceived solutions. Such rubber-stamp solicitations will invariably backfire and leave people more distrusting and cynical than ever.

If the leaders do not see inclusion as a way to create better and more deployable strategies that are fully owned by the organization, then it is better to stick to traditional top-down, cascading approaches and accept their inherent ineffectiveness.

Playing the Strategy Game

If strategists don't play chess anymore because it is too analytical and constrained to meet today's challenges—as mentioned at the beginning of this book—what games do we play?

True strategists are capable of playing what we call massively multiplayer online role-playing games, or MMORPGs for short. These are played at an order of magnitude of more—more journeys, more environments, more freedom of "moves," and more people working together who have never met one another.

True strategists think and act differently to reclaim strategy and turn it into a more engaging and rewarding experience. Instead of being a periodically run, burdensome direction-setting exercise, strategy becomes an ongoing source of inspiration and energy. And when they are no longer whiplashed by constant change, managers can see and take advantage of what's coming and align the organization accordingly.

The most important message from this book is that strategy is back—so much so that we don't need a game that resembles strategy. We have one. It's called business.

Appendix

The History of Strategy

THIS BOOK CONTAINS MANY QUOTES from literature and publications concerning strategy that helped us make the case for reclaiming strategy. These resources also served a broader purpose as the essential inspiration for finding answers to two questions: What happened to strategy to make it much less of a factor in a company's success? What can be done now to *fix it* and make strategy relevant again for today's organizations?

We answered both questions within a framework of noteworthy publications that ultimately supported our conclusions and allowed us to formulate a way forward for reclaiming strategy. In these closing pages, we use these same sources to provide a general overview of where strategy has been, the predicament it is in now, and where it can be taken.

Strategy Formulation and Implementation Baseline

For the vast majority of its history, business strategy was fairly boring, as economic activity tended to focus on exclusivity and monopolies.

Exclusivity Strategies: Up to 1900

In the Middle Ages, the exclusive right to levy taxes or charge tolls was a key source of strategic advantage. Tradesmen organized themselves in guilds to regulate who was allowed to perform services and the conditions under which those services could be performed. Heavily protected trade routes to the Far East brought the Dutch VOC (Vereenigde Oostindische Compagnie), or Dutch East India Company, great wealth in the 1700s. In the United States, the railway companies had a strong grip on economic activity and were among the most important companies whose shares traded on stock exchanges (although fortunes were both won and lost). Monopoly and exclusivity strategies proved so effective that entire countries were colonized and many wars were fought over them. To this day, the exclusivity that a patent for a powerful drug provides is an attractive proposition, albeit more difficult to achieve.

Ida Tarbell's 1904 book, *The History of the Standard Oil Company*, signaled the transition to a new strategic era. Tarbell depicted John D. Rockefeller as a money-grabber who was viciously effective at monopolizing the oil trade. Rockefeller had gradually expanded his control over the refining business by taking over competitors. It is said that Rockefeller vanquished competitors by opening up his financial ledgers. When competitors saw that Standard Oil was selling its product at a profit, although its price was well below their own production costs, they were eager to sell. It is estimated that at one point, Standard Oil and its 30 wholly and partially owned subsidiaries controlled more than 90 percent of North American refinery capacity.

The company exerted so much control over oil refining and distribution that it was deemed too successful and potentially damaging to the development of other industries. Yet, although the Standard Oil experience turned the United States and much of the world against monopoly strategies, the company's operational prowess proved to be a harbinger of things to come.

Industrial Proficiency Strategies: 1900–1968

Pushing the boundaries of industrialization and operations marked the strategic space over the next 60 or so years. Frederick Winslow

Taylor, with his 1911 monograph "The Principles of Scientific Management," marked the beginning of modern organizational thinking with a focus on industrial operations. In 1931, under the sponsorship of Alfred P. Sloan, the man who made General Motors into one of the largest industrial corporations on earth, the first university-based executive education program—the Sloan Fellows program—was launched at Massachusetts Institute of Technology (MIT). Through a Sloan Foundation grant, the MIT School of Industrial Management was established in 1952 and given a mandate to educate the "ideal manager." The school was later renamed the Alfred P. Sloan School of Management.

This period also saw the birth of many of the premier consultancies that are still active today. Tellingly for this period, they were often referred to as "business engineers."

By the early 1960s, the word *strategy* was commonly used in business, with the publication of books such as *The Theory of the Growth of the Firm* by Edith Penrose in 1959, *Strategy and Structure* by Alfred D. Chandler, Jr., in 1962, and *Managing for Results* by Peter Drucker in 1964.

At the time—the decades after World War II—big oligopolistic bureaucracies were dominant. As Michael Hammer and James Champy explain in *Reengineering the Corporation*:

> The regimes of Robert McNamara at Ford, Harold Geneen at ITT, and Reginald Jones at General Electric epitomized management of that era. Through elaborate planning exercises, senior managers determined the businesses in which they wanted to be, how much capital they should allocate to each, and what returns they would expect the operating managers of these businesses to deliver to the company. Large staffs of corporate controllers, planners, and auditors acted as the executives' eyes and ears, ferreting out data about divisional performance, and intervening to adjust the plans and activities of operating managers.

The concept of strategy that Chandler and Drucker envisaged was mainly focused on what the firm itself had to do to secure its long-term future, particularly the actions and the allocation of resources needed to achieve the desired results. The role of competition was still a relatively minor element. But that soon changed.

The Heyday of Strategy: 1969 to the Mid-1990s

In the late 1960s and early 1970s, Bruce Henderson, who later founded the Boston Consulting Group, published works on the "experience curve," the idea that there is a direct relationship between cumulative production and production costs.

Author and journalist Walter Kiechel wrote about this in *The Lords of Strategy* in 2013:[1]

> The experience curve was, simply, the single most important concept in launching the strategy revolution. . . . What the experience-curve concept did was to instigate a sea change in the way companies think about their costs. . . . Its basic truths . . . when first proclaimed were electrifying: businesses should expect their costs to decline systematically, at a rate that can be accurately predicted. . . . A bigger market share typically means you have more experience—you've made more of the product—which should mean your costs are lower than theirs. (*Get big or get trounced.*) . . . With the experience curve, the strategy revolution began to insinuate an acute awareness of competition into the corporate consciousness.

If competition was hardly a factor in the early 1960s, two decades later, it had become almost the whole ballgame. "The essence of strategy formulation," declared Michael Porter in 1979 in his first landmark article for *Harvard Business Review* ("How Competitive Forces Shape Strategy") and his 1985 book, *Competitive Advantage: Creating and Sustaining Superior Performance*, "is coping with competition."

Porter's premise was that "the essence of formulating competitive strategy is relating a company to its environment." The key aspect of the environment was the industry the company is in and that industry's structure. As Kiechel noted in *The Lords of Strategy*, the framework posited five factors that were essential to determining how profitable an industry could be for its players and where and how a company within it might have room to compete.

Porter's framework offered a more complete picture of the forces of competition. Essentially, three strategies emerged: low-cost leadership (the company wins on price), product differentiation (the company charges more for a distinctive product), and market specialization (the company dominates a market niche).

Five years later, in their *Harvard Business Review* article, "The Core Competence of the Corporation" (1990), C. K. Prahalad and Gary Hamel highlighted the need not only to look at positioning in terms of markets and competitors, but also to look inside one's own company. Cynthia Montgomery and David Collis connected the resource-based view of the firm to its positioning in their 1995 *Harvard Business Review* article, "Competing on Resources: Strategy in the 1990s." Thus, the debate between inside-out strategies and outside-in strategies was never a real debate. Both mattered.

Strategy became a proper discipline during this period—more stand-alone, more analytical, and more cerebral—and thus was less of a daily task for senior executives and more the responsibility of strategy professionals and planners. This had the unwanted side effect of creating a distinct handover between strategy creation and strategy activation, with all of the accompanying issues. The more sophisticated and sweeping strategies became, the larger the handover hurdles.

As executing strategy turned into a major endeavor, organizational buy-in and change management became much-discussed topics. Experts were churning out advice on how to turn strategies into competitive rubber meets the road, or how to create an organization that would be conducive to making the new strategy happen. By the early 1990s, business was coming to grips with organizational change through books such as *Leading Change* by John P. Kotter in 1996.

Change management had become a true discipline that was closely linked to strategy.

By the mid-1990s, everything was lined up to put brilliant strategies to work. But, in retrospect, companies had very little time to enjoy the full set of strategic tools and approaches. The house of strategy was about to be disrupted.

Disruptive Overload

In 1997, Clayton Christensen wrote about disruptive innovation in *The Innovator's Dilemma*. Unlike incremental innovation, which steadily led to better products, disruptive innovation led to cheaper and somewhat inferior products that steadily took market share. This would go on until incumbents finally reacted. But they were often too late. Although some of Christensen's case examples have been criticized—some of the companies he names were doing remarkably well 10 years after the disruption, and some of the disruptor companies failed—his mechanism for disruptive innovation left a trail of fundamentally changed businesses and industries.

The majority of the turmoil was attributed not to Christensen's concept, but to disruption in general. Christensen wrote the book in the language of vertically integrated businesses selling products and services, while most disruptive innovations were played out at the value chain level, where they disrupted not only industries but also strategy on a profound scale.

In 1993, Michael M. Hammer and James Champy published *Reengineering the Corporation: A Manifesto for Business Revolution*. They rightly identified an abundance of opportunities to rethink the processes of companies, especially in view of automation and later digitization. Cheaper versions of processes were springing up to help companies make their business more competitive, and often disruptively so. Suddenly, there was a trend so big that it couldn't be ignored, and it didn't fit into any of the existing strategy frameworks. The reengineering revolution had hijacked the strategy process.

But the reengineering wave did not last long. By the late 1990s, the next strategic shift had arrived, drawing us all into the big promise of the Internet and the new economy. In 1999, *Blown to Bits: How the New Economics of Information Transforms Strategy* by Philip Evans and Thomas S. Wurster made a convincing argument that the Internet had changed everything. Now disintermediation and disintegration were possible for just about anything, putting intermediaries and vertical integration seriously at risk. The impact of such disruptive innovation at the value chain level was profound.

By this time, it was obvious that the Internet had provided a huge boost, allowing companies to create LEGO-block-style value chains or completely networked enterprises. The breakup of the vertically integrated business was upon us; this is best told in "Unbundling the Corporation," a 1999 *Harvard Business Review* article by John Hagel III and Marc Singer.

It was never a question of which strategic shift was the most important or which would trigger the most disruptive innovation; rather, it was the fact that the shifts were piling up, each one bringing with it plenty of opportunities to create or lose competitive advantage. The Internet, globalization, big IT, technology, social communities, and even the global financial crisis: each one was here to stay, and they cumulatively provided new strategic degrees of freedom. Thomas L. Friedman's 2005 book, *The World Is Flat: A Brief History of the Twenty-First Century*, drove home the message that resources, markets, and competition are global and operating on an increasingly level playing field.

Technology also led to disruptively new ways of tapping into resources. In their 2006 *Harvard Business Review* article, "Connect and Develop: Inside Procter & Gamble's New Model for Innovation," Larry Huston and Nabil Sakkab wrote about how Procter & Gamble was turning developers inside and outside the company into a seamless development capability, showing how distributed capabilities were becoming mainstream.

Social technologies were becoming a breeding ground for new community services such as peer-to-peer lending, product and service recommendations in hospitality and travel, and a host of other areas. The global financial crisis was a source of profound and sudden business dynamics, illustrating that some external events are bigger than anyone can imagine or anticipate. The crisis heightened an interest in ways to deal systematically with global risks and triggered many publications, including the 2010 republishing of *Black Swan: The Impact of the Highly Improbable* by Nassim Nicholas Taleb.

Many other major shifts had become stand-alone strategic considerations, as outlined in *The War for Talent* by Ed Michaels, Helen Handfield-Jones, and Beth Axelrod; *Hypercompetition* by Richard D'Aveni; and *Big Data: A Revolution That Will Transform How We Live, Work, and Think* by Viktor Mayer-Schönberger and Kenneth Cukier. But then this is exactly what has typified the past two decades. There were many excellent concepts, recipes, and frameworks for dealing with one or maybe two disruptive strategic shifts, but no overriding framework to pull it all together.

Who Needs Strategy, Anyway?

The steady stream of strategic shifts appeared to make strategy irrelevant. It was so easy to see new and better ways to operate and to create competitive advantage that everybody was in pursuit of these with no time to waste. It almost didn't matter which new sources of competitive advantage were to be won, as long as the company capitalized on enough of them fast enough. And because almost everyone was facing the same situation, there was nothing short of a competitive stampede.

Strategy also became more complicated, further eroding any chance it had to step in as a guiding force in a competitive maelstrom. With every new strategic shift, strategy formulation became a little more complex, as more interrelated factors had to be considered. The resulting strategic complexity reached a point where it overpowered regular strategic frameworks and analyses. There was simply no spreadsheet or framework that was big enough or comprehensive enough to analytically accommodate all the strategic parameters and possible permutations.

Strategy had become so overly complex that companies seemed not to need it anymore. As Walter Kiechel, author of *The Lords of Strategy*, observed in an interview a few years ago, "It's tough to identify any big new strategy ideas since 1995."

As companies faced a growing list of urgent initiatives, a point was reached where there were more strategic initiatives than could be handled—even to stay at par with the competition. Immersed in day-to-day urgencies, companies gradually lost their internal sense of purpose and direction.

"Ersatz Strategies": Dealing with the Unwanted Side Effects

As strategy tools and concepts became overwhelmed, so did organizations and their leaders. But strategic headway had to be made. Fortunately, the situation encouraged many bright strategic thinkers to come up with answers.

Authentic Leadership and Corporate Values

Strong, authentic leadership and powerful corporate values providing clear direction are appealing to every organization. And when companies are facing tumultuous business environments, the prospect of genuine leadership looks decidedly magical. The past decade has seen a proliferation of publications and professional services supporting effective leadership. A good place to look for inspiration is *HBR's 10 Must Reads on Leadership* by Peter F. Drucker et al., from 2011.

No Regrets Tactics

Even in the absence of a clear and guiding overall strategy, it was still possible to pursue strategic initiatives of the "no regrets" type. *Lean*

Six Sigma (2002) and *Lean Six Sigma for Service* (2003) by Michael L. George, for example, brought together the Six Sigma approach (developed by Motorola in 1985 and embraced by Jack Welch for GE in 1995) and lean concepts to minimize waste, taking the strategy beyond manufacturing. Lean Six Sigma offered a stand-alone concept with its own goals, metrics, approaches, and training.

Customer centricity and loyalty continued to be prominent goals. Who could argue that having more customers who are true ambassadors for your products and services is not good for business? For this reason, the net promoter score, as laid out in the 1996 book *The Loyalty Effect: The Hidden Force Behind Growth, Profits, and Lasting Value* by Frederick F. Reichheld and Thomas Teal, enjoyed considerable attention, and still does to this day.

Benchmarking continues to be popular and widespread, as learning from successful players has a very straightforward logic to it. Numerous books have focused on the practice. The inspirational benchmarks were most interesting to strategists, who generally preferred to go beyond the immediate operational and organizational treats. *The Toyota Way: 14 Management Principles from the World's Greatest Manufacturer* (2003) by Jeffrey Liker and *Good to Great: Why Some Companies Make the Leap . . . and Others Don't* (2001) by Jim Collins are among the best.

Strategic Relief

If strategy formulation had become more complex because of the proliferation of strategic variables, then it made sense to narrow the field. A variety of useful ideas could be found in the best practices of successful companies. *Profit from the Core: Growth Strategy in an Era of Turbulence* (2001) and *Repeatability: Build Enduring Businesses for a World of Constant Change* (2012), both by Chris Zook and James Allen, provided an effective way to focus on a subset of strategic parameters. *Good Strategy/Bad Strategy: The Difference and Why It Matters* (2011) by Richard Rumelt was a very different way to make strategy more digestible. *Blue Ocean Strategy* (2005) by W. Chan Kim and Renée Mauborgne suggested that focusing on finding uncontested market space is a rewarding form of strategy formulation. Many other smart ways to bring the overall strategic challenge down to more manageable—though arguably sometimes oversimplified—proportions have also been suggested.

Agility, Flexibility, and Resilience

A last resort (but also a useful approach to finding strategic relief) is to acknowledge that formulating lasting strategies in a constantly changing environment has become so difficult that it should not even be attempted. The answer must instead be sought in strategic agility, organizational flexibility, and resilience. This way, you not only keep up with change but also take advantage of fundamental shifts faster than the competition does. *Fast Strategy: How Strategic Agility Will Help You Stay Ahead of the Game* (2008) by Yves Doz and Mikko Kosonen and the 2013 blog entry "The Agility Factor" by Thomas Williams, Christopher G. Worley, and Edward E. Lawler III offer examples of strategic agility in response to rapidly changing environments.

New Approaches to Management

Traditional bureaucratic organizations are ill equipped to deal with today's dynamic business environments. Set up to ensure stability, productivity, and top-down control, they are almost the opposite of what is needed.

New Management

Fast-changing business environments necessitate new approaches to management. The requirements for this are easy to define: the shift of power toward customers requires more focus on delighting customers, developing new and more innovative ideas, and experimenting to find out quickly what works and what doesn't. While a great deal of research and thinking has gone into these new management approaches, one thing is certain: instead of seeking proof from the past, companies will have to rely on new forms of integrative and design thinking, and on abductive logic that asks the what-if questions. There is a growing number of books, articles, and TED Talks in the marketplace that delineate the principles and practices of this approach, which are fundamentally different from those of hierarchical bureaucracy. They all go well beyond discussions of new technologies, fixes, and tweaks. Here is a short list of our favorites: *The Leader's Guide to Radical Management* (Stephen Denning), *Fixing the Game* (Roger Martin), *What Matters Now* (Gary Hamel), *Reorganize for Resilience* (Ranjay Gulati), *The Power of Pull* (John Hagel, John Seely Brown, and Lang Davison), *The Innovator's Prescription* (Clayton Christensen et al.), *The Leader's Dilemma* (Franz Röösli et al.), *Conscious Capitalism* (John Mackey and Raj Sikodia), *Peak* (Chip Conley), *The Lean Startup* (Eric Ries), *The Ultimate Question 2.0* (Fred Reichheld et al.), *Wiki Management* (Rod Collins), *The Elastic Enterprise* (Nicholas Vitalari and Haydn Shaughnessy), *Flat Army* (Dan Pontefract), *The Connected Organization* (Dave Gray), *Reinventing Giants* (Bill Fischer et al.), and *Big Bang Disruption* (Larry Downes and Paul Nunes).

There is no doubt that organizations will move to new management approaches in the years ahead. But, as highlighted in many of the publications listed here, there are several caveats to consider. For one thing, the shift will not be one of "new firms" versus "old firms"; instead, new ways of operating are likely to coexist with the old ways, even in the same organization. This is easiest to understand when we think of the back office of a bank holding millions of customer accounts or airline pilots who must follow strict instructions and safety protocols. Also, while a focus on customers, innovation, and experimentation is useful in figuring out what works and what doesn't in some environments, it is not a substitute for strategy, especially when it comes to making "bet-the-company" billion-dollar investments. The biggest caveat is that strategy tends not to have an explicit role. New ways of management and a strong focus on customers and innovation are somehow expected to save the day.

Mission Command

The military has always faced considerable near-future uncertainty. Helmuth von Moltke, chief of the Prussian (later German) general staff in 1857, explains it this way: "No plan of operations extends with any degree of certainty beyond the first encounter with the main enemy force."

To cope with uncertainty, von Moltke developed and applied the concept of *Auftragstaktik* (literally, "mission tactics"), a strategic approach that stressed decentralized initiatives within an overall strategic design. He argued that the uncertainties of war make it unlikely that perfect plan-of-force alignments could be mapped out in advance of a mission. He believed that, after calculating the initial mobilization and concentration of forces, leaders needed to make decisions based on a fluid, constantly evolving situation.

In the twentieth century, von Moltke's thinking became more influential, and by the 1980s it was the preferred style for exercising military command and had become the formal doctrine of the U.S. Army: *Mission Command* (ADRP 6-0, Department of the Army, Washington, DC, 2012).

The purpose of mission command is to reduce uncertainty throughout the organization. Leaders work closely with their people to codevelop a vision, ensure that this vision is well communicated and widely understood, and manage a set of strategic missions to accomplish the vision. They delegate authority for decision making to those levels that can acquire and process information and move into action quickly, without waiting for detailed orders. It is an inclusive approach that makes full use of an organization's talent, offers more flexibility, and improves understanding and commitment throughout the organization (see *Mission Command*, U.S. Army, 2003).

Interestingly, at the same time that the military was abandoning the top-down, information-based approach to strategy in favor of mission command principles, strategists in business were embracing the old ivory towers. This was unfortunate because business was about to become a whole lot more uncertain.

Competitive Life Cycles

In business, it is useful to think about strategy in terms of an ongoing portfolio of competitive opportunities (strategic missions) rather than a single formula spun over a multiyear cycle. In her 2013 book, *The End of Competitive Advantage: How to Keep Your Strategy Moving as Fast as Your Business*, Rita Gunther McGrath argues that competitive advantage is no longer sustainable and that it has a life cycle. To be successful, she says, requires learning to initiate, grow, capitalize on, and say goodbye to competitive advantage, all in due time.

This notion of fast-fleeting competitive advantage does not come as a big surprise. In fact, most organizations have learned to adapt to this reality and often have many—sometimes too many—strategic initiatives running at any given time in an attempt to sustain their overall competitiveness.

There is one crucial conclusion to be derived from Gunther McGrath's work: if competitive advantages are indeed transient and have life cycles, the organization will need to have more of them in parallel, and will need to manage them as a portfolio with interdependencies. If this is done, when some of them have run their course, new ones will be ready to take their place.

Several recent publications discuss ways to take practical advantage of managing nonfinancial portfolios. In "Rebalance Your Initiative Portfolio to Manage Risk and Maximize Performance" (*Harvard Business Review* report, 2008), Peter LaCasse talks about the importance of managing strategic initiatives as a portfolio with interdependencies and tracking the impact that the initiatives have on one another. In "Manage with a Portfolio Mindset" (*Harvard Business Review* Blog Network, 2012), Ron Ashkenas explains why portfolio management is not just a financial management concept, but is equally applicable to other groups of interrelated things that need to be managed.

The idea of a portfolio of competitive opportunities makes strategy something that is managed on an ongoing basis. It breaks up the single large strategic sequence into multiple more nimble minisequences at different stages of development, held together by an overriding portfolio management concept: a company's strategic game plan.

Even the traditionally grand scheme, strategy, launch, and business-plan-focused startups have big appetites for continuous approaches to creating competitive advantage. In *The Lean Startup: How Today's Entrepreneurs Use Continuous Innovation to Create Radically Successful Businesses* (2011), Eric Ries demonstrates that an earlier and more granular approach for testing hypotheses in the market allows startups to get early feedback on what works and what doesn't so that they can create a more attractive proposition in less time. In his 2013 *Harvard Business Review* article, "Why the Lean Start-Up Changes Everything," Steve Blank declares that lean startup principles are also valid for corporations and argues that corporations should step away from a single, perfect business plan.

Organizational Inclusiveness

In his epic book *The Innovator's Dilemma* (1997), Clayton M. Christensen argued that larger organizations with strong vested interests in ongoing businesses were ill equipped to capitalize on disruptions. This is unwelcome news now that disruptions have become a fact of life.

Fortunately, the same disruptive technologies also provide solutions. Armed with the latest collaborative and social technologies, people are able to contribute to their company's success, more so than ever before. In his *Harvard Business Review* article "Accelerate!" (2012), John P. Kotter discusses the value of such an approach and how a shadow organization made up of willing coalitions of people can help drive the company's strategic frontiers. This is the best of both worlds: independent initiatives that secure the future for the organization while simultaneously drawing on the best the organization has to offer. Kotter also observes that individuals can be readily motivated to participate in such coalitions.

An explanation for why this works can be found in research into organizational motivation by, among others, Dan Pink in his 2009 TED Talk "The Puzzle of Motivation" and Dan Ariely in his 2012 TED Talk "What Makes Us Feel Good About Our Work?" Research shows that motivation works very differently for mechanical tasks and for tasks that require even minimal cognitive efforts. Mechanical tasks can be motivated by money. But this isn't true for cognitive tasks, where the motivating factors include autonomy (having some say about the outcome), mastery (having a sense of personal growth), and purpose. As it happens, all these boxes are checked by giving people the freedom to tackle strategic issues and opportunities with like-minded coworkers. People not only help determine the outcome, but also learn and grow and help repair the disenfranchisement that comes from indiscriminately chasing competitive advantage.

Drawing In the Future

In their 2007 *Harvard Business Review* article, "A Growing Focus on Preparedness," Darrell Rigby and Barbara Bilodeau reported that the use of scenario planning had increased markedly since 2002, coinciding with a general renewed interest in future-focused tools, techniques, and services. The reason, they said, is that we humans intuitively understand that in a faster-changing environment, where we begin tells us little about where we will end up. In other words, when we are developing strategies, we need to shift the emphasis, moving from what we know about our point of departure to what we know about the future. This is true even if the point of departure is thoroughly understood.

Another interesting perspective is design. In a 2008 *Harvard Business Review* article, "Design Thinking," Tim Brown offers several perspectives on designing innovative products and services. One perspective is particularly valuable in formulating strategy: Brown talks about bringing innovations in products, services, and even business models to the next level by developing them within a multidisciplinary setting that incorporates user inspiration. The fundamental shifts affecting users directly fuel the innovation process. This does a number of things: it creates a longer innovation horizon, it improves the innovations, and it makes those innovations easier to implement because of the multidisciplinary involvement—all of which sounds like something that strategy could use right now.

When these two perspectives—scenario planning and design thinking—are combined, strategy creation becomes integrally linked to the future rather than to the here and now.

Going Forward: Reclaiming Strategy

Strategy needs to be turned from an incomplete competitive game plan into a driving organizational energy. With any luck, 10 years from now, we will talk about the period of reclaiming strategy that started in the mid-2010s of this century. This is an altogether more attractive outlook than reaching the conclusion that real strategy had a life span of only a few decades.

Notes

Introduction

1. John P. Kotter, *A Sense of Urgency* (Boston: Harvard Business School Press, 2008).

Chapter 1

1. Thomas Friedman, "THINK: A Forum on the Future of Leadership," IBM Centennial, New York, September 20–21, 2011.
2. Richard N. Foster and Sarah Kaplan, *Creative Destruction: Why Companies That Are Built to Last Underperform the Market, and How to Successfully Transform Them* (New York: Currency/Doubleday, 2001).
3. Gary Hamel, "Strategy as Innovation," *Harvard Business Review*, 1996.
4. *Mobile Navigation Services and Devices*, 6th edition, Berg Insights AB, April 2013.
5. Larry Downes and Paul Nunes, *Big Bang Disruption: Strategy in the Age of Devastating Innovation* (New York: Penguin, 2014).
6. Ibid.
7. Roger L. Martin, *The Design of Business: Why Design Thinking Is the Next Competitive Advantage* (Boston: Harvard Business Press, 2009).
8. Ibid., pp. 128–129.
9. In war gaming, participants play themselves, competitors, regulators, and new entrants amid external shocks such as regulatory change or technological disruption.

Chapter 2

1. Gary Hamel, "Moon Shots for Management," *Harvard Business Review*, February 2009.
2. Robert Greene, Joost Elffers, *The 33 Strategies of War* (New York: Penguin, 2014). Kindle edition.
3. M. Handschuh et al. "Optimization from the Middle," A.T. Kearney, 2013.
4. Daniel Pink, *Drive: The Surprising Truth About What Motivates Us* (New York: Riverhead Books, 2009).
5. Osvald Bjelland and Robert Chapman Wood, "An Inside View of IBM's Innovation Jam," *MIT Sloan Management Review*, October 1, 2008.

6. U.S. Army, Field Manual *Mission Command: Command and Control of Army Forces*, Headquarters Department of the Army, 2003.

Chapter 3

1. Peter Drucker, *Managing for Results* (New York: Harper & Row, 1964).
2. A.T. Kearney Strategy Study, August 2013.
3. Rita Gunther McGrath, *The End of Competitive Advantage: How to Keep Your Strategy Moving as Fast as Your Business* (Cambridge, MA: Harvard Business School Press, 2013).
4. *How Increased Competition from Generic Drugs Has Affected Prices and Returns in the Pharmaceutical Industry*, Congressional Budget Office Report, July 1998.

Chapter 4

1. Lawrence Freedman, *Strategy: A History* (Oxford, U.K.: Oxford University Press, 2013), p. 9.
2. This case study is based on lessons learned during FutureProof strategy projects at several organizations. For confidentiality reasons, the identities of the firms have been disguised and the strategic insights and conclusions have been selectively represented.

Chapter 5

1. This quote by American computer scientist Alan Kay became the early-days hallmark of Xerox Palo Alto Research Center (PARC) when it famously invented the graphical user interface and the first true personal computer, the Alto. PARC, in effect, predicted the course of the digital revolution. "The Debriefing: John Seely Brown," *Wired*, Issue 8.08, August 2000.
2. Nicholas Vitalari and Haydn Shaughnessy, *The Elastic Enterprise* (Longboat Key, FL: Telemachus Press, 2012).
3. "J.C.Penney: Was Ron Johnson's Strategy Wrong?," *Forbes*, April 9, 2013.
4. "Rapid-Fire Fulfillment," *Harvard Business Review*, November 2004; "When Will US Firms Become Agile? Part 2: Internal Agility at Zara," *Forbes*, September 20, 2012.
5. "Fashion Forward," *The Economist*, March 24, 2012.

Chapter 6

1. Robert Greene, *The 48 Laws of Power* (New York: Penguin Books, 2000), p. 60.
2. This is 48 percent higher than it was 12 months earlier, compared to the S&P 500 gain of 18 percent.
3. "Adobe's Bold Embrace of the Computing Cloud Should Inspire Others," *Economist*, March 22, 2014.

4. Ibid.
5. "Is Adobe's Bold Move Setting It Up to Be Disrupted?," *Forbes*, March 28, 2014.
6. "Newton (Platform)," Wikipedia, note 7, http://en.wikipedia.org/wiki/Newton _(platform).
7. The simplified version of Moore's law says that processing power for computers will double every two years.
8. "Google+ Is the Fourth Most-Used Smartphone App," *Business Insider*, September 5, 2013.

Chapter 7

1. Helmuth von Moltke, quoted in S. Bungay, *The Art of Action: How Leaders Close the Gaps Between Plans, Actions, and Results* (Boston: Nicholas Brealey Publishing, 2011), Kindle edition, locations 1686–1688).
2. John P. Kotter, *A Sense of Urgency* (Cambridge, MA: Harvard Business School Press, 2008).

Appendix

1. *The Lords of Strategy* describes the rise of the large strategy consulting firms— BCG, McKinsey, and Bain—and the business school professors who contributed conceptual frameworks and pragmatic insights to the strategy revolution. Kiechel, a former managing editor at *Fortune* magazine, was the editorial director of Harvard Business Publishing from 1998 to 2002.

Index

Page numbers followed by *f* and *t* refer to figures and tables, respectively.

About the Authors

Johan Aurik is A.T. Kearney's managing partner and chairman of the board, a role that he took on in January 2013. Previously, Johan served as the firm's regional head for Europe, the Middle East, and Africa. Prior to that, he was the unit leader for the Benelux region, a member of A.T. Kearney's board of directors, and head of the consumer goods and retail practice in Europe.

Johan joined the firm in 1989 and has worked in North America and Europe. He has more than 25 years of consulting experience with A.T. Kearney in the consumer, retail, chemicals, and transportation industries. His areas of expertise include strategy and market effectiveness, organizational design, complexity, and supply chain management.

Johan is the author of numerous articles and the coauthor of *Rebuilding the Corporate Genome* (John Wiley & Sons, 2002). In 2013, he was named one of the "Top 25 Consultants" by *Consulting* magazine. He holds master's degrees in history from the University of Amsterdam and from the Johns Hopkins University School of Advanced International Studies.

Dr. Martin Fabel is an A.T. Kearney partner and global head of the firm's strategy practice. Martin has more than 20 years of consulting and industry experience serving clients in the communications, media, consumer, retail, and various service industries worldwide with a focus on Europe and the Middle East.

His areas of expertise include corporate and business unit strategies, go-to-market designs, digital marketing, e-commerce, and comprehensive marketing and sales transformations.

Between his first term at A.T. Kearney from 1993 to 1998 and rejoining the firm in 2003, Martin was head of the entertainment, media, and commerce division of a leading European live entertainment provider. He earned his doctorate in journalism and communication sciences from Freie Universität Berlin and a master's degree in business administration.

Gillis Jonk is an independent strategy consultant and business innovator. He helps organizations turn major business trends and discontinuities into competitive advantages, while providing the *foresight* to allow them to pursue audacious and game-changing goals. He was previously a partner in A.T. Kearney's strategy practice and chair of the firm's Global Knowledge and Innovation Council. His areas of expertise include business  and competitive strategies, innovation, value chain strategies, root cause analyses, inclusive strategy development, and organizational design and motivation.

Gillis is the author of numerous articles and is coauthor of *Rebuilding the Corporate Genome* (John Wiley & Sons, 2002). He earned his MSc in mining engineering from Delft University of Technology, Netherlands, and an MBA from the Rotterdam School of Management, Erasmus University, Netherlands.

About A.T. Kearney

A.T. Kearney is a leading global management consulting firm with offices in more than 40 countries. Since 1926, we have been trusted advisors to the world's foremost organizations. A.T. Kearney is a partner-owned firm that is committed to helping clients achieve immediate impact and increase their advantage on their most mission-critical issues. For more information, visit www.atkearney.com.